Alaska Travel Guide

2023-2024

A Family-Friendly Guide to Hidden Gems, Historic Towns, and Beachside Escapades

Michelle K. Cordell

Table of Contents

INTRODUCTION

Alaska, which is located in the extreme northwest of North America, is a monument to the magnificence of nature. For years, adventurers, nature enthusiasts, and people looking for peace have been enthralled by this unique state's towering mountains, cold glaciers, immaculate coastlines, and untamed wilderness.

Enter the heart of the Last Frontier on a journey via this 2023–2024 travel guide to Alaska. Making your Alaskan dreams come true is the only goal. Whether you're a seasoned traveler or a first-timer, see this gorgeous country's wonders. The idea is to provide a method to visit Alaska that is welcoming, humanized, and uncomplicated so that you may fully appreciate its magic.

Visualize yourself admiring the majestic animals in their natural surroundings or watching the mesmerizing Northern Lights dance over the Arctic skies. Picture yourself admiring the massive Denali, North America's tallest peak, or taking a cruise along the picturesque Inside Passage. Everything is here and prepared for you.

However, Alaska is home to much more than just breathtaking scenery. It has a bustling culinary scene, a robust culture, and a rich history that has all been shaped by the diverse local and immigrant cultures that have inhabited the area. You can explore Alaska's many adventures with the aid of the guide, including dining on the best seafood and making friends with native Alaskans.

You'll discover helpful information and travel advice as you browse through these sections to assist you in planning your Alaskan journey. You are taken care of in every way, from organizing your trip and learning the ideal times to go to know how to stay safe in the environment and take in the state's fascinating history.

So without further ado, let's embark on a once-in-a-lifetime journey. You are drawn to the majestic land filled with grizzlies and glaciers. This book will be your dependable travel companion as you cross this enormous wilderness and create enduring experiences in the Last Frontier. Alaska, with all its wonders, is waiting to be explored. Here in the center of Alaska, where the wonders of nature and interactions with people are waiting, your trip begins.

Chapter 1: Welcome to Alaska's Wonders!

Greetings from the amazing state of Alaska, a place full of untamed beauty and natural wonders where the sky is painted a different shade of unfathomable splendor every daybreak. This travel guide will be your reliable companion as you discover the wonders and mysteries of the 49th state.

This is a path that requires letting go of complexity and embracing simplicity. Alaska's immense wilderness, untamed coastlines, and genuine adventures entice visitors. Here, family vacations turn into treasured memories, undiscovered jewels beckon, and historic villages hum with historical tales.

These pages unveil the mysteries of Alaska's shore attractions and provide priceless travel advice, stunning itinerary ideas, and the delights of family travel. The tour guide leads visitors to immaculate beaches, medieval towns where time appears to stand still and exhilarating outdoor sports.

Jargon is substituted with simple, approachable language in this journey through Alaska, making it possible for all visitors experienced or not to fully understand the spirit of this amazing region. Alaska is more than just a location; it's also a sensation, an encounter, and an adventure that must be shared.

So let's put the complexity behind us, enter Alaska's unadorned, breathtaking beauty, and create lifelong memories in the Land of the Midnight Sun.

Chapter 2: Reaching Alaska's Majestic Landscapes

Getting to Alaska's magnificent scenery is simpler than you would imagine. It's like having a large nature-filled road vacation, but in the sky, by sea, or on land.

Traveling to Alaska is a little like going to see a good friend, only your buddy is a whole state packed with beauty. No need for intricate planning here; nature in Alaska is ready to embrace you with open arms. So let's make accessing these gorgeous places as easy as a walk in the park.

Flying into Alaska

Arriving in Alaska, particularly if it's your first visit, seems a little like walking into a world of natural beauties. You jump on a plane, and before you know it, you're surrounded by Alaska's jaw-dropping vistas.

As you gaze out of the aircraft window, you'll be met with the sight of snow-capped mountains, huge woods, and exquisite lakes. It's not a terrifying voyage; in fact, it's more like walking into a dream.

Whether you're a seasoned traveler or a newcomer, flying into Alaska is like opening the first page of an intriguing novel. You're about to go on a magnificent journey, and the world of Alaska is your intriguing narrative.

Navigating the Waters to Alaska

Getting to Alaska is an interesting experience that might also include going by boat. This means you have the choice of witnessing the gorgeous Alaskan coastline, a trip worth every second.

Many travelers opt to cruise to Alaska, and it's a great way to explore. Cruise liners provide a unique vantage point, enabling you to view the raw beauty of the Alaskan coastline from the luxury of your vessel.

From the deck, you'll stare at the majestic glaciers, and fjords, and possibly even glimpse animals like whales or sea lions. It's not simply a form of transportation; it's an extraordinary experience that links you personally with Alaska's coastal marvels. So, whether you're flying above or cruising alongside, your visit to Alaska is a fantastic chapter in your travel adventure.

Overland Adventures to Remember

Traveling to Alaska by land is a great adventure, a fascinating chapter in your trip. It's about hitting the open road and experiencing the untamed environment of this large state.

You may opt to drive, soaking in the gorgeous views at your speed. There's a distinct delight in drifting across Alaska's picturesque roadways, with every twist and bend unveiling nature's treasures. Just be ready for probable interactions with animals, from moose to bald eagles.

Or you may choose for the rail trip. The Alaska Railroad provides an extraordinarily gorgeous path across the state. Sit back in your comfy seat, stare out of the window, and let the breathtaking panoramas unroll before your eyes.

Whether by automobile or by rail, your overland experience in Alaska will be carved in your mind forever. It's about exploring the heart of this region, taking the path less traveled, and immersing oneself in the raw beauty of Alaska.

Chapter 3: Crafting Your Alaskan Journey

Planning your Alaskan adventure is like crafting a painting. It's about picking what you want to see and experience. Whether you're attracted to the rough wilderness, ancient cities, or coastal beauty, you're the artist, and Alaska is your canvas.

Don't hurry; take your time to paint your schedule with the colors of your passions. Maybe you want to start with animal encounters, add a touch of glacial beauty, or weave in some local culture. It's all up to you.

Remember, your path is unique, and there's no right or wrong way to accomplish it. It's all about what gets you thrilled and intrigued. So, create your Alaskan experience, and let it be a reflection of your interests and ambitions.

Finding the Perfect Time to Explore

Picking the ideal time to visit Alaska is like picking the finest moment to eat a ripe grape. It's all about finding the right blend of nice weather and exhilarating experiences.

Summer, from June to August, is when Alaska comes alive. The days are long, and you may savor outdoor activities like hiking, fishing, and animal watching. But remember, it's also the peak tourist season, so popular places might become packed.

Shoulder seasons in May and September provide a calmer, more budget-friendly experience. The weather may be a little more unpredictable, but you'll get the opportunity to explore Alaska's splendor without the rush and bustle.

And if you're up for a different type of enchantment, try the winter months. From late September to mid-April, the Northern Lights dance over the Alaskan sky. It's a captivating natural display you won't want to miss.

In the end, it's about picking the time that matches your tastes. Whether you choose the brightness of summer or the calm-of-shoulder seasons, Alaska has plenty to offer throughout the year.

Ensuring Safety and Respecting Wildlife

Safety and wildlife respect in Alaska are like watching out for your closest buddy. You want to keep them secure while enjoying your time together.

1. Wildlife Watching Etiquette: When you observe Alaska's magnificent wildlife, keep a polite distance. It's like giving someone personal space. Keep at least 25 yards from most animals and 100 yards from bears and their cubs. It's like giving them liberty to wander.

2. Bear Safety: Just as you secure your front door, carry bear spray. It's your safety blanket. Learn how to utilize it appropriately. Hiking or camping? Make noise, like chatting or clapping, to let bears know you're approaching. It's like ringing the doorbell.

3. Outdoor Gear: Dress properly for the weather. Think of it as dressed to impress Alaska's nature, that is. Layers are your best friends, like comfortable sweaters in winter. And don't forget sturdy footwear for those outdoor pursuits.

4. Remain Informed: Watch out for the weather conditions conjecture. It's like checking your phone for updates. Also, know where you're going and inform someone of your intentions - much like sending a message when you're going out with buddies.

5. Emergency Kit: Carry a tiny kit with necessities like a first aid box and food. It's like having an extra charger you hope you won't need it, but it's nice to have.

6. Leave No Trace: Imagine you're a visitor at a friend's home. Clean up after yourself. Don't litter. Treat Alaska's scenery as you would your house with care.

Respecting animals and remaining safe in Alaska is all about knowing and respecting this magnificent environment while looking out for your well-being. It's like creating a relationship, a mutual respect where everyone appreciates the trip.

Where to Rest Your Head in Alaska

Choosing a location to lay your head in Alaska is like selecting the comfiest space in your own house. It should feel exactly perfect, and there are alternatives for everyone, whether you're on a limited budget or searching for a touch of luxury.

Budget-Friendly Stays

1. **Hostels:** Think of them as your homey college dormitories. They give a bed and frequently a communal kitchen and common room. Perfect for travelers on a budget who appreciate meeting other adventures.

2. **Cabins & Cottages:** These are like tiny homes away from home. You receive a private place with some basic conveniences. Great for people who desire a rustic experience.

Mid-Range Comfort

1. Hotels: Just like renting a stay at a well-known brand, Alaska has a fair amount of hotels. You receive a nice bed, room service, and all the normal hotel amenities.

2. Lodges: These are like boutique hotels located in gorgeous surroundings. They frequently provide rustic charm paired with contemporary comforts.

Luxurious Retreats

1. Resorts: Imagine a tropical beach resort, but in the center of the Alaskan wilderness. Resorts provide everything from spa services to gourmet food. It's luxury at its best.

2. Wilderness Lodges: These are like walking into a private Alaskan wonderland. They give top-notch service and frequently have private cabins and unique activities.

Camping

1. Camping Sites: If you like outdoor experiences, camping in Alaska is like sleeping beneath the stars in your garden. Many places offer minimal amenities.

2. RV Parks: If you have an RV, these are like owning a mobile home. It's a terrific way to experience Alaska at your leisure.

Just like your house, where you choose to stay in Alaska should reflect your style. Whether it's a tiny hostel bed or a sumptuous resort suite, you'll find a place to lay your head that meets your style and budget. It's all about making your Alaskan vacation distinctly yours.

Cruising and Commuting in Alaska

Getting around Alaska is an experience in itself. From sailing on the open oceans to commuting along picturesque roads, you'll discover numerous ways to experience this magnificent region.

Cruising Along the Coast

1. Alaska Marine Highway: Think of this as the Alaskan equivalent of a road trip, but on the sea. Hop on a boat to ride around the coastline, experiencing the magnificent fjords and islands.

2. Luxury Cruises: These are essentially floating resorts that transport you to wonderful places. Enjoy fine dining, entertainment, and, of course, breathtaking views from your balcony.

Scenic Commutes

1. Rail Travel: Picture yourself on a classic train journey through Alaska. The rail routes pass through jaw-dropping landscapes, making the journey as memorable as the destination.

2. Road Trips: Rent a car or an RV and hit the Alaskan highways. You'll feel like you're on your mobile adventure, with captivating scenery outside every window.

3. Bush Planes: In the remote reaches of Alaska, you may get on a tiny aircraft, like your very own private transport, to visit locations that are impossible to reach by road.

Alaska's immense environment is made to be explored, and there's a transportation choice for every sort of tourist. So, whether you're cruising the beaches, riding the rails, or on a typical road trip, you'll discover that getting about is just as interesting as the places themselves.

Chapter 4: Discovering Alaska's Unique Charms

Alaska's got some wonderful things to offer. Ever heard of Denali? It's the largest mountain in North America, towering tall and proud. Then there's the wildlife, like those gigantic grizzly bears and gorgeous bald eagles. Even humpback whales came by for a visit. And as the night falls, the Northern Lights light up the sky, it's like a celestial art exhibition. Plus, the seaside beauty here is off the charts. Imagine glaciers meeting the water, and you sailing through the Inside Passage, surrounded by beautiful rainforests, totem poles, and quaint tiny communities. Nature's got its A-game on in Alaska, and it's all here for you to explore.

Must-See Destinations

When you're in Alaska, there are certain locations you simply can't miss. First up, Denali National Park, it's like the kingpin of national parks, with its huge peaks and immense wildness. Then there's Glacier Bay, where you'll witness those massive glacier masses meeting the water. You'll desire to get a look at Wrangell-St. Elias too. it's the largest national park in the U.S. and a playground for explorers. Don't overlook the Arctic National Wildlife Refuge, a magnificent natural beauty.

Now, the Tongass National Forest, that's where you'll discover old rainforests, so lush they're like nature's cathedral. But what's going to blow your mind? The Northern Lights. When the night sky dances with such brilliant hues, it's like enchantment. And when you need a break from all that raw beauty, stop via the Inside Passage, where tiny coastal communities will charm your socks off. So, yep, you've got some major investigating to do!

Immersing in Denali National Park

Ah, Denali National Park - get ready for an adventure in the rugged heart of Alaska. When you go into this region, it's like entering a huge, undisturbed forest where nature prevails.

You'll find yourself surrounded by huge mountains, notably the big kahuna, Denali itself. It's the tallest mountain in North America and a stunning stunner. Then there's the wildlife grizzly bears, moose, caribou, and more. Imagine witnessing these gorgeous animals in their natural environment!

But what makes Denali especially special? It's all about the sensation of being little in this huge, untamed area. You may climb, camp, or just take a bus trip to bask in the jaw-dropping scenery. Just remember, it's not about conquering nature here; it's about honoring and enjoying it. So, be ready to enjoy the wild side of Alaska!

Wildlife Encounters: Alaska's Treasures

Alaska's wildlife is like a living treasure box, waiting to be unearthed. Think of it as a real-life animal kingdom. It's where you may view nature's best, up close and personal.

Here's your opportunity to glimpse the titans of the north grizzly bears rumbling through the wilderness, moose calmly nibbling on greens, and caribou herding like they've got a great parade planned. And let's not forget the magnificent bald eagles, the cautious owls, and the lovely sea otters.

What's the trick to experiencing these treasures? Patience, respect, and a decent set of binoculars. The pleasure of seeing a bear from a safe distance or an eagle poised on a treetop is something you'll never forget.

Just remember, while you're out there, you're a visitor in their house. So, walk softly, take only memories, and leave just footprints. Alaska's animals will reward you with memories that'll remain with you forever.

Gazing at the Northern Lights

The Northern Lights, nature's light show, a celestial dance that covers the night sky with dazzling hues. It's like seeing magic develop right over you.

As you stand there, staring at the Northern Lights, you'll experience a sensation of amazement, like a kid looking up at the sky. It's a moment of pure magic, shared with the cosmos itself. You'll want to record it in your mind forever.

So, when the night is clear and the lights make their appearance, walk outdoors, gaze up, and let yourself be captivated. The Northern Lights are Alaska's gift to the world, a reminder of the beauty that surrounds us.

The Coastal Allure of Alaska

The Alaskan shore is a site where land and water join together in a magnificent embrace. The sound of waves smashing against craggy cliffs, the salty wind in your hair. it's an experience that links you to nature's raw, untouched beauty.

As you explore Alaska's shore, you can glimpse playful otters or spectacular whales breaching the surface. The beach teems with life, from tiny crabs scuttling along the rocks to majestic eagles swooping above. It's a live, breathing ecosystem, a reminder of the fragile balance of nature.

So, when you find yourself on the seaside in Alaska, take time to smell the salty air, feel the sand under your toes, and let the rhythm of the waves calm your soul. This is where land and water join, and you become a part of the coastal allure that is distinctly Alaskan.

The Magic of the Inside Passage

The Inside Passage, a magnificent miracle of nature, spreads before you like pages in a storybook. Picture it: serene, gleaming seas bordered by towering evergreen woods, a relaxing voyage through a coastal paradise.

Imagine yourself on a boat, quietly sailing over these lovely seas. The air is crisp, with just a tinge of the sea's salty flavor. Surrounding you are fjords, coves, and islands, each one presenting a different experience. You could notice playful seals lazing in the sun, or perhaps even a pod of orcas, nature's magnificent black and white giants.

The Inside Passage is a passageway of surprises, each curve in the coastline revealing something new. Hidden waterfalls stream from lush, green cliffs, as old glaciers gently make their way to the sea. As you cruise, you'll witness attractive coastal communities and their colorful dwellings dotting the landscape, like valuable diamonds along the beach.

So, if you find yourself cruising through the Inside Passage, make sure to stand on deck and take in the fresh air. Feel the peacefulness of the moment, let the stunning landscapes surround you, and remember that here is where nature's magic takes center stage, and you are the charmed audience.

Chapter 5: Thrilling Outdoor Pursuits

Lace-up your boots, wear your outdoor gear, and answer the call of Alaska's wild side. In this area of your Alaska travel guide for 2023-2024, it's all about the outdoors, adventure, and the excitement of discovery.

Introducing the incredible adventures that await, whether you're conquering mountains, kayaking across beautiful lakes, mushing with a team of huskies, or reeling in that coveted fish. In simple words, it's here to assist you in delving headlong into fascinating Alaskan outdoor pastimes and let you in on the secrets to make the most of your journey. Whether you're a seasoned outdoors lover or fresh to the game, you're covered.

The lure of the wild calls, and Alaska's magnificent vistas are your playground. It's time to explore the Last Frontier in all its magnificence. Get ready to build experiences that will last a lifetime and take home tales you'll be discussing for years to come. The journey starts now.

Mush into Adventure with Dog Sledding

Experience the excitement of dog sledding in the gorgeous Alaskan tundra. Picture yourself flying over a beautiful snowy landscape, escorted by a squad of eager Alaskan huskies. This isn't simply a ride; it's a profound connection with the heart of Alaska.

Explore the wonderful world of dog sledding. The purpose is to deliver plain, accessible information. You don't need to be an expert; This tutorial will help you understand why dog sledding is such a riveting Alaskan trip.

Also covers what you can anticipate, how to prepare, and what to be wary of, ensuring you're completely equipped for your dog sledding excursion. Whether you're a first-timer or an expert musher, this guide has you covered.

Beyond the practical techniques, you'll uncover the remarkable relationship between mushers and their magnificent canine partners. These canines are more than athletes; they're your buddies on this Alaskan trip.

Prepare to mush across Alaska's magnificent landscapes, experiencing the force of the sled and the warmth of these wonderful dogs. Create memories that will last a lifetime on this memorable vacation.

Soar Above the Scenic Beauty with Helicopter Tours

Alaska's gorgeous vistas are famous worldwide and for a good reason. To properly understand the immensity and magnificence of this untamed border, one must ascend to the sky. Helicopter tours give a thrilling method to accomplish precisely that, and in this area of the Alaska travel guide, we will study the art of flying above this beautiful splendor.

Helicopter excursions in Alaska are meant to make the state's beautiful scenery accessible to everyone. Age and physical health don't restrict your possibilities to explore the Last Frontier from a thrilling viewpoint. These trips are great for anybody wanting an adventure with a bit of wonder.

This chapter will lead you through the fundamentals of helicopter trips in Alaska. It explains what to expect, how to prepare for your vacation, and the wonderful vistas you'll experience. The language is straightforward and unadorned since understanding and enjoying these excursions should be easy and pleasurable.

Helicopter trips are not only about transport; they're about change. You'll take in vistas that few get to experience: glaciers that have persisted for millennia, towering mountains that touch the sky, and possibly even sightings of Alaskan animals in their native environment. This is not simply a trip; it's an emotional experience that unites you with the wild beauty of Alaska.

Whether you're a first-time visitor or a seasoned tourist, these trips will leave an everlasting impact on your Alaska experience. Prepare to be taken to the sky, where the landscape underneath becomes a living masterpiece and your connection to this wonderful country increases.

Witness the Majesty of Whales

Witnessing the magnificence of whales in Alaska is an incredible experience. Alaska's clean seas are home to many marine creatures, including these gentle giants. This part of the Alaska travel guide looks into the wonderful world of whale watching. Here, It provides a detailed image of what to anticipate while seeing these wonderful animals.

Alaska's waterways host seasonal whale migrations, with the Inside Passage and Southeast Alaska being recognized for outstanding whale-watching possibilities. The finest season is frequently summer when you may watch humpback whales, orcas, gray whales, and more. Learn about their habits and ethical whale-watching procedures, creating a genuine connection with these amazing species.

Choosing a trustworthy whale-watching excursion is crucial. Their guide gives suggestions and insights for an amazing experience with Alaska's whales. Your tour in the Last Frontier will be enhanced by these unique moments.

Paddle Through Pristine Waters: Kayaking

Kayaking across Alaska's pristine waterways is an amazing activity that gets you near nature's unadulterated splendor. In this segment of our Alaska travel guide, we examine the delights of kayaking and how you may make the most of this experience.

Alaska's wide landscapes provide many paddling options. From quiet lakes and beautiful bays to demanding rivers and fjords, there's something for kayakers of all ability levels. Whether you're a seasoned kayaker or a rookie, Alaska's waterways offer an experience for you.

This book gives insights into some of the greatest kayaking places, such as Kenai Fjords National Park, Prince William Sound, and Glacier Bay. Get ready for interactions with animals, including seals, otters, and eagles. This book offers gives information on safety and gear, ensuring you're well-prepared for your kayaking excursion.

With kayaking, you'll not only enjoy the calm of Alaska's outdoors but also get a greater understanding of the state's pristine ecology. Your kayaking vacation in Alaska will be a memory you treasure forever.

Hike & Backpack in Alaska's Vast Wilderness

Alaska's immense environment is a hiker's dream. This part of the Alaska travel guide goes into the exhilarating world of hiking and backpacking, enabling you to see the pristine beauty of the Last Frontier.

From rocky mountain paths to calm woodlands, Alaska has a wealth of hiking and backpacking possibilities. Hikers of all levels will discover paths that fit their interests. Whether you're a seasoned traveler aiming to climb a hard mountain or a casual hiker seeking a pleasant walk, these paths appeal to every explorer.

This section presents some of Alaska's most prominent hiking sites, such as Denali National Park, Kenai Fjords, and the Chugach State Park. Expect breathtaking panoramas, animal interactions, and the peacefulness of nature as you venture on these paths.

Additionally, you'll get crucial recommendations on safety, gear, and Leave No Trace principles to guarantee your hiking and backpacking trips are not only fun but also ecologically responsible.

Whether traveling over a glacier, through a lush forest, or along the coastline, hiking and backpacking in Alaska gives you a chance to interact with the state's untamed environment like no other experience.

Camping and RVing: Nature's Embrace

Alaska is a mecca for outdoor enthusiasts, and camping in the center of its unspoiled wilderness is an experience like no other. This part of our Alaska travel guide digs into the benefits of camping and RVing, enabling you to immerse yourself in nature's embrace.

Camping in Alaska: Whether you're an experienced outdoors person or a newbie camper, Alaska provides a broad choice of camping alternatives. From established campsites with facilities to remote camping where you can fully unplug, you'll discover the right location to pitch your tent. Iconic destinations like Denali National Park, Kenai Fjords, and Chugach State Park appeal with their magnificent splendor. Wake up to the sounds of nature, breathe in the fresh, pure air, and view Alaska's stunning scenery from your campground.

RVing in Alaska: For those who enjoy a bit of luxury while still delighting in the great outdoors, RVing is a wonderful alternative. Alaska's wide road network makes it suitable for RV excursions. Cruise along magnificent byways like the Alaska Highway, the Seward Highway, or the Top of the World Highway, stopping at RV-friendly campsites along the route. Your RV becomes your home on wheels, allowing the freedom to explore the Last Frontier at your speed.

Wild Camping: If you're seeking isolation and adventure, Alaska is also renowned for wild camping. In many regions, you may pitch up camp in the forest, far from the trappings of modern life. However, with this freedom comes immense responsibility. Respect the environment, practice Leave No Trace principles, and be well-prepared when you journey into the vast parts of Alaska.

Tips & Essentials: This gives information on important camping gear, safety in bear territory, campfire etiquette, and the Leave No Trace principles. These suggestions guarantee that you not only have a pleasant camping experience but also help the preservation of Alaska's natural environment.

Camping and RVing in Alaska enable you to disconnect from the rush and bustle of everyday life, allowing an opportunity to reconnect with nature, create lasting memories, and experience the untamed beauty of the Last Frontier. This section gives the information and tools you need to begin your expedition into Alaska's wild heart.

Reaching New Heights: Mountaineering

Alaska's towering peaks and unknown lands allure individuals with a hunger for adventure and a passion for reaching the highest summits. Delves into the realm of mountaineering, where enthusiasts rise to unprecedented heights and test the frontiers of human accomplishment.

Hard Summits: Alaska features some of North America's most hard and rewarding summits. From the legendary Denali, the highest peak in North America, to lesser-known treasures like Mount Foraker and Mount Logan, there are summits to enchant mountaineers of all abilities. Whether you're a seasoned pro or a newbie climber, Alaska's summits offer various routes and experiences.

Mountaineering in Denali National Park: Denali is a hotspot for mountaineers. The national park around the mountain offers a clean setting, with rocky terrain and unpredictable weather. To climb Denali is to embark on a genuine adventure. Whether you join a guided expedition or explore solo, reaching the top of this mammoth peak is a pinnacle moment in every mountaineer's journey.

The Alaska Range: This powerful mountain range provides several hard ascents. The technical skill necessary to ascend peaks like Mount Hunter and Mount Huntington is equaled only by the pure joy of gaining the top. The Alaska Range's craggy spires and stunning glaciers inspire climbers from throughout the globe.

Preparation and Safety: This gives insights into necessary mountaineering gear, preparation advice, and safety measures. Safety in the unpredictable Alaskan environment is vital, and thorough preparation is necessary for a successful climb. Understanding the specific difficulties and needs of Alaska's mountains assures a safe and enjoyable trip.

Local Expertise: Many travelers opt to climb Alaska's peaks under the supervision of local mountaineering specialists. Their expertise in the landscape, weather patterns, and safety issues may substantially improve your experience. We give ideas for guide services to make your climb smoother and more pleasurable.

Conquering Alaska's Peaks: Mountaineering in Alaska is not only about climbing peaks; it's about stretching your limitations, connecting with the raw force of nature, and embracing the spirit of discovery. This section offers you the information and motivation to begin your climbing expedition in the stunning landscapes of the Last Frontier. Whether you're conquering one of Alaska's legendary peaks or traveling off the usual route, this is your guide to achieving new heights in the world of mountaineering.

The Thrill of Catching Fish in Alaskan Waters

Alaska's seas teem with life, providing fishermen with an unmatched fishing experience. This section looks into the world of fishing, where scenic rivers, lakes, and coastal locations offer the background for remarkable encounters with some of the world's most sought-after species.

Renowned Fishing Grounds: Alaska's rivers and lakes are renowned among fishermen. The state's streams are home to five kinds of salmon: king (chinook), silver (coho), sockeye (red), pink (humpy), and chum (dog). In addition to salmon, the state has trophy-size halibut, trout, grayling, and northern pike. These waterways give fishermen infinite choices and make Alaska a fishing paradise.

The Salmon Flow: Witness the yearly salmon flow, a natural phenomenon that's as awe-inspiring as it is legendary. Every year, millions of salmon return to their birthplaces to spawn and finish their life cycle. This event not only sustains Alaska's fishing economy but also allows fisherman the chance to test their talents against one of the ocean's mightiest beasts.

Variety of Fishing types: Whether you like fly fishing in tranquil river settings or deep-sea angling for record-sized halibut, Alaska supports all fishing types. From ice fishing in the winter to casting in the midnight heat of July, there's a strategy for every season and fish type.

Local Fishing Knowledge: Gain insights into local fishing charters and guides who can assist you in traversing Alaska's vast and varied fishing terrain. These specialists know the finest sites and strategies to enhance your chances of pulling in the catch of a lifetime.

Regard for Nature: Emphasize the necessity of responsible fishing and a profound regard for Alaska's ecosystem. Sustainable fishing techniques guarantee these waterways remain rich in life for centuries to come. Understanding catch limits, seasonal limitations, and catch-and-release ethics is crucial to sustaining Alaska's amazing fish populations.

Epic Tales and Memories: Fishing in Alaska isn't just about the excitement of the catch; it's about the tales and memories produced in the process. Whether you're reeling in a king salmon or releasing a wild trout, each minute spent by Alaska's waterways is a gift.

Angler's Paradise: From isolated wilderness fishing adventures to more accessible angling chances near cities and towns, Alaska provides limitless alternatives for both seasoned and beginner fishermen. This section will help you equip up and be ready to start on an exciting excursion into Alaska's world-class fishing zone.

In this area of rocky coasts, wild rivers, and tranquil lakes, you're welcome to explore the excitement of fishing in Alaska. Come prepared to create your own epic fishing stories and experience the amazing beauty of the state's natural surroundings.

Chapter 6: Shopping Finds on the Last Frontier

Discover Alaska's distinctive retail environment. From local art to delectable seafood and outdoor gear, this tour uncovers the many shopping delights of the Last Frontier. Explore local handicrafts, find souvenirs, and indulge in gastronomic pleasures. Don't forget to explore local galleries and antique stores for unusual items. Alaska's shopping experiences are as varied as its landscapes, each with a touch of the state's character and beauty.

Native Artistry and Handicrafts

In Alaska, the art isn't simply something you witness; it's a physical link to the state's profound cultural traditions. You'll discover chances to meet local craftsmen, hear their tales, and even try your hand at some of these time-honored skills. Whether it's the expressive masks of the Tlingit people, the magnificent patterns of the Athabascans, or the vibrant prints of the Inuit, you'll be intrigued by the range and ingenuity of Alaska's native craftsmanship.

Alaska's native handicrafts aren't simply art; they frequently contain spiritual value, revealing tales of their past, the natural environment, and the people who have made this region home for decades. This book gives insights on where to acquire these gems, assuring you take home not just a stunning piece of art, but a piece of Alaska's history.

So come along and let the native craftsmanship and handicrafts of Alaska fascinate you, linking you to the traditions and history of this magnificent region.

Savor the Bounty of Alaskan Seas

Alaska's culinary sector is as varied and rich as its scenery. While in the state, experience the wonderful wealth of Alaskan waters. The beautiful seas of Alaska provide a plethora of seafood, making it a must-visit destination for seafood enthusiasts.

Salmon, halibut, king crab, and other indigenous species take a major place in Alaskan cuisine. Whether eating in a sophisticated restaurant or relishing a basic seafood shack meal, you'll taste the fresh, clean flavors of the ocean. Pair your dinner with a local craft beer or a great wine, and you have the ideal combination for a memorable dining experience.

But it's not just about the fish. Alaska's gastronomic joys extend to wild animals such as moose, reindeer, and caribou, as well as foraged items including berries, mushrooms, and wild greens. Exploring this gourmet trip is a vital aspect of knowing the state's culture and traditions.

This travel guide will introduce you to the most amazing eating venues, from fine-dining seafood restaurants to tiny neighborhood cafes. Navigate the menus and enjoy the greatest Alaskan food. So, don't just visit Alaska; taste it and fall in love with the state's extraordinary culinary riches.

Equipping for the Outdoors: Gear and Apparel

Equipping for your Alaskan expedition involves careful consideration of the distinct outdoor circumstances. When it comes to clothing and clothes, being prepared is vital to a safe and pleasurable vacation. Whether you're exploring the rough environment, trekking the beautiful trails, or starting on a fishing adventure, having the correct kit may make all the difference.

The basics for outdoor activities in Alaska include:

1. **Layered Clothing:** The climate in Alaska may fluctuate greatly. Layered clothing is crucial to adjust to changing weather. Start with moisture-wicking base layers, add insulating layers, and end with waterproof and windproof upper layers.

2. **Quality Footwear:** Durable, waterproof boots are vital, particularly if you want to walk or explore damp terrains. Don't forget moisture-wicking socks to keep your feet dry and comfortable.

3. Backpack: A comfortable, waterproof backpack is necessary for carrying basics like water, food, a first-aid kit, and additional clothing.

4. Hiking and Camping Gear: If you're intending to hike or camp, you'll need a strong backpack, a trustworthy tent, a warm sleeping bag, and a portable stove for cooking.

5. Safety Equipment: Items like a compass, a headlamp, a multi-tool, and a first-aid kit are vital for your safety.

6. Binoculars and Cameras: Alaska's magnificent scenery and animals make it a paradise for photography and wildlife observation. High-quality binoculars and a camera are fantastic extras.

7. Fishing Gear: If you're a fisherman, evaluate the sort of fishing you expect to undertake and carry the necessary rods, reels, lines, and lures.

8. Bear protection Equipment: If you're touring a bear area, bear spray, and bear-resistant food containers are vital for your protection and the bears'.

9. Insect Repellent: Alaskan summers may bring out the bugs, so bringing good insect repellent is recommended.

10. Personal Items: Don't forget necessities like sunscreen, sunglasses, a hat, and a reusable water bottle.

This travel guide includes recommendations on where to purchase the finest outdoor gear and clothes, ensuring you're well-prepared for your Alaskan journey. Enjoy your exploration of the Last Frontier with peace of mind, knowing you have the necessary tools at your disposal.

The Allure of Local Handmade Treasures

Exploring the distinct appeal of Alaskan native handmade goods is a fun element of your tour through the Last Frontier. Alaska's creative community is vast and diversified, providing a broad assortment of handmade objects that make for fantastic memories or presents. When you choose to support local craftspeople, you're not only bringing home a piece of Alaska but also helping to the preservation of its unique culture.

Here are some of the local handcrafted wonders you may discover:

1. **Native Alaskan Art:** Alaska's indigenous cultures have a long legacy of making art that represents their history and relationship to the land. Look for wonderfully constructed totem poles, delicate ivory carvings, and brilliant beading.

2. **Jewelry:** Alaskan jewelers typically combine materials from the state's natural beauty into their designs. From gorgeous gold nugget jewelry to pieces using local gemstones, there's something for everyone.

3. **Fiber Arts:** Alaskan craftsmen are excellent at crafting warm and unusual clothing items, including handcrafted knitted or woven products like scarves, mittens, and sweaters.

4. Baskets & Weavings: Native Alaskan tribes are noted for their exquisite basket weaving and grass weaving skills, resulting in gorgeous and utilitarian objects.

5. Ceramic & Ceramics: Alaskan artisans manufacture stunning ceramics inspired by nature. Handcrafted mugs, bowls, and vases typically reflect the state's natural beauty.

6. Woodwork: Local woodworkers make beautiful and utilitarian objects like hand-carved spoons, bowls, and elaborate wooden art.

7. Stained Glass: Artists combine parts of Alaska's nature into stained glass masterpieces, generally representing views of the outdoors and animals.

8. Art Galleries: Many communities in Alaska are home to art galleries presenting a diversity of local talent. These are fantastic sites to locate unique and one-of-a-kind works of art.

9. Quirky gifts: Don't forget to discover quirky, entertaining, and unusual gifts that express the essence of Alaska, from comical moose-themed things to Alaskan-themed calendars.

As you examine these treasures, you'll have the opportunity to meet the artists, learn about their creative processes, and get a greater understanding of Alaska's culture. These handcrafted souvenirs will not only remind you of your Alaskan journey but also make for meaningful and unique presents for your loved ones.

Souvenirs to Remember

Bringing home keepsakes from your Alaskan excursion is a fantastic way to treasure the memories of your journey. These souvenirs reflect the spirit of the Last Frontier and make for unique recollections or considerate presents for friends and family. When you search for mementos, you're not simply getting baubles; you're collecting elements of Alaska's character.

1. Handmade Arts and Crafts: Native Alaskan art and crafts are exceptional souvenirs. Look for beautifully crafted totem poles, intricate ivory carvings, beaded

jewelry, and baskets that carry the spirit of Alaska's indigenous cultures.

2. Alaskan Wildlife-Themed Items: Alaskan wildlife is diverse and captivating. You may get souvenirs depicting moose, bears, eagles, and more. Consider purchasing stuffed animals, sculptures, or even apparel with nature themes.

3. Alaskan Seafood: Alaskan seafood is famous. Bringing back smoked salmon, canned salmon, or even salmon jerky is not only a great keepsake but also a lovely opportunity to share a taste of Alaska with others.

4. Gold Rush Memorabilia: Relive the thrill of the Gold Rush period with souvenirs including gold nugget jewelry, gold rush-themed novels, and even little vials of actual Alaskan gold.

5. Local Art: Alaskan artists portray the state's magnificent environment in their paintings and pictures. You may discover art that showcases the huge vistas, colorful sunsets, and the stunning Northern Lights.

6. **Local Handicrafts:** Items such as hand-carved wooden bowls, totem pole replicas, and woven baskets represent the craftsmanship of Alaska's indigenous people.

7. **Unique Alaskan apparel:** From comfortable sweaters and scarves to T-shirts with funny moose or bear motifs, Alaskan-themed apparel is both utilitarian and a fun keepsake.

8. **Birch Syrup and Jams:** Birch syrup is a distinctly Alaskan sweet delicacy. You may also discover delectable jams prepared from the state's bountiful berries.

9. **Alaskan-Themed Calendars and Books:** Educational and artistically spectacular, these goods may bring a bit of Alaska into your house.

10. **Alaskan-Made Soaps and Candles:** These items frequently incorporate natural ingredients and smells inspired by Alaska's outdoors.

11. Quirky, Fun, and Offbeat Items: Don't forget to investigate quirky, amusing, or odd mementos. Look for products that represent the character of the state, such as moose-themed mugs, hilarious Alaskan sayings, or even whimsical bear-themed décor.

By bringing home these mementos, you're not simply taking home physical recollections of your Alaskan vacation; you're also sharing the wonder of Alaska with your loved ones. Each item tells a unique tale of your trip in the Last Frontier.

Art Galleries and Craft Shops: Local Artistry

Alaska is a country of enormous natural beauty, and it has also inspired a flourishing artistic sector. Exploring local art galleries and artisan stores is a fantastic opportunity to appreciate the creativity and skill that lives in the Last Frontier. Whether you're an art enthusiast or just a lover of beautiful things, you'll discover a richness of creative expression in Alaska.

Local Art Galleries

1. Anchorage Museum: The Anchorage Museum is a center for Alaskan art and culture. You'll discover a broad assortment of modern and traditional Alaskan art here. The museum also displays touring exhibitions.

2. Alaska Native Heritage Center: This center is not only a location to learn about Alaska's indigenous traditions but also to view and buy original Native Alaskan art, from complex beading to magnificent sculptures.

3. worldwide Gallery of Contemporary Art (IGCA): Located in Anchorage, IGCA displays cutting-edge contemporary art from Alaskan and worldwide artists. It's a location to study current creative creations.

4. Artique Ltd.: Situated in Anchorage, Artique Ltd. is an artist-owned gallery that provides a variety of art styles. You may find anything from paintings and sculptures to jewelry and ceramics.

Craft Shops

1. Alaska Native Arts Foundation: This business in Anchorage specializes in real Native Alaskan art and crafts. It's a fantastic spot to discover handcrafted handicrafts that represent indigenous cultures.

2. Makushin Valley Arts Center: Located in Dutch Harbor in the Aleutian Islands, this arts center is a terrific site to explore unique local arts and crafts, frequently reflecting the sea and animal environs.

3. The Juneau Artists Gallery: In Juneau, this cooperative gallery displays the work of local artists. You may discover varied things, including paintings, sculptures, jewelry, and more.

4. Fairbanks Arts Association: This gallery in Fairbanks shows a vast variety of art mediums, including paintings, photos, textiles, and jewelry, all made by local artists.

5. Talkeetna Roadhouse Mercantile: In the picturesque hamlet of Talkeetna, this boutique provides diverse

Alaskan-made items, from knitwear and artwork to soaps and jams.

Supporting local artists and crafters is not only a way to bring a bit of Alaska's creativity into your life but also a means to appreciate the variety of the state's creative skills. Whether you're looking for a unique artwork for your house or a tiny, handmade memento, these galleries and artisan businesses will expose you to the bustling world of Alaskan craftsmanship.

Unearth Antiques and Unique Discoveries

Exploring Alaska's antique stores and unique boutiques may be a pleasant trip through history and local workmanship. Here are some areas to find antiquities and rare treasures in the Last Frontier:

1. Anchorage

Antique Malls: Anchorage features various antique malls, such as the Brass Rabbit and Fireweed Antique Mall. These treasure troves contain a diverse variety of antiquities, from old furniture to collectibles.

Oomingmak Musk Ox Producers' Co-Operative: For unique and handmade products, visit this co-op where Alaska Native women manufacture wonderful qiviut (musk ox down) knitwear, such as scarves and caps.

2. Fairbanks

Alaska Antique facility: Located in Fairbanks, this facility is a sanctuary for antique aficionados. You may discover a diversity of stuff including ancient maps, vintage jewelry, and Alaskan artifacts.

A Fine Store: This boutique provides an outstanding assortment of gifts, including high-quality jewelry, glassware, and regionally inspired goods.

3. Talkeetna

Nagley's shop: A historic general shop in the center of Talkeetna, Nagley's is noted for its varied products. You may find antiques, literature, and unique Alaskan souvenirs.

Flying Squirrel: This eccentric business is recognized for its antique and retro products. You'll discover everything from apparel to housewares, typically with an Alaskan twist.

4. Juneau

Juneau Artists Gallery: Besides featuring local art, this gallery offers various arts and crafts, including ceramics, glasswork, and wood creations. A fantastic site to discover unique handcrafted goods.

5. Kenai Peninsula

Old Inlet Bookstore: Located in Homer, this bookstore specializes in secondhand and rare books. If you're a book fan, you'll enjoy searching the shelves for literary gems.

6. Seward

Seward Salamander: This delightful business is a sanctuary for unusual and Alaskan-themed goods. You may get anything from artisan jewelry to funny gifts.

Exploring these vintage stores and boutiques not only enables you to find hidden gems but also helps local companies. Whether you're hunting for an antique jewel, a unique Alaskan gift, or just want to take in the history and culture, these businesses provide a fascinating view into the Last Frontier's rich past and innovative present.

Chapter 7: Entertainment and Nighttime Delights

Alaska's nightlife provides different activities, from live music to cultural acts, gaming, and local hangouts. Enjoy live performances, view the Northern Lights, taste cultural dances, try your luck at local gaming, attend events and festivals, laugh at comedy clubs, feast on Alaskan cuisine, explore craft breweries, and find local hangouts. Alaska's nights are as remarkable as its days.

The Sounds of Alaska: Live Music and Bars

Alaska's live music and bar scene is a mesmerizing world of sound where local and international performers join together to give you fantastic nights. From soulful jazz to rocking blues and modern hits, these live performances cover a broad spectrum of music genres. Whether you're a lover of private acoustic sessions in warm pubs or swaying to the newest sounds in lively music venues, Alaska's music culture offers something for everyone. So, get out, enjoy the local culture, and let the rhythms of Alaska accompany your evenings out.

Gazing at the Night Sky: Northern Lights

Gazing at the night sky in Alaska promises the possibility of viewing one of Earth's most spectacular occurrences — the Northern Lights. These magnificent curtains of light, often known as the Aurora Borealis, delight the skies, painting the darkness with bright colors. They're a heavenly dance that leaves observers in wonder. To see this ethereal vision, go away from city lights, especially in the winter months, and be patient. Northern Lights are a natural phenomenon that can't be hurried. But when they come, it's an event that will remain with you forever.

Cultural Performances That Inspire

Alaska's cultural acts give a glimpse into the rich past of this state. The indigenous tribes here have tales to tell, and they convey them via dance, music, and art. These performances typically integrate traditional and modern elements, giving you a feel of the developing Alaska. You could watch elaborate dances symbolizing the link to nature or hear melodies that mimic the spirit of the country. These cultural experiences serve as a bridge between the past and the present, and they're a chance to develop a greater knowledge of Alaska's indigenous peoples.

Roll the Dice: Casinos and Gaming

Alaska may not be the first destination that springs to mind when you think of casinos and gambling, but it does offer some unusual possibilities for those who prefer trying their luck. While the state doesn't have regular casinos with slot machines and table games, it does offer an innovative sort of gaming entertainment: charity gaming. Charitable gaming comprises activities like bingo and pull-tab games, and they're generally conducted by charitable groups. These games are a fun way to test your luck while donating to worthy organizations. It's crucial to know that Alaska has rigorous rules and regulations governing gambling, so make sure to engage properly and within the legal limitations. So, if you're in the mood for some gaming fun with a charity twist, Alaska offers a unique option.

Celebrate Like a Local: Events and Festivals

When visiting Alaska, immerse yourself in the local culture by celebrating like a native at the various events and festivals that take place throughout the year.

1. Fur Rendezvous: Held in Anchorage in late February, this festival comprises several winter-themed festivities, including the legendary Running of the Reindeer. It's a terrific way to experience Alaska's winter spirit.

2. Iditarod Trail Sled Dog event: The famed dog sledding event begins in Anchorage and concludes in Nome. If you're in Alaska in early March, seeing the ceremonial start in Anchorage is a must.

3. Summer Solstice Festival: On June 21st, Anchorage conducts a Summer Solstice Festival, marking the longest day of the year. Enjoy live music, cuisine, and local artisans.

4. **Alaska State Fair:** Running from late August to early September, this fair in Palmer provides a real Alaskan experience with agricultural displays, music, rides, and distinctive Alaskan delicacies.

5. **Alaska Day Festival:** Held in Sitka on October 18th, this festival marks the official transfer of Alaska from Russia to the United States. Enjoy parades, reenactments, and local food.

6. **Alaska Native Heritage Center Celebrations:** Throughout the year, the center offers events to exhibit the diverse cultures and traditions of Alaska's indigenous peoples. You may enjoy traditional dances, paintings, and storytelling.

7. **Arctic Entries:** This storytelling event, hosted in Anchorage, is a unique chance to hear personal experiences from Alaskans. It's like a local version of TED Talks.

8. **Kodiak Crab Festival:** If you're on Kodiak Island around Memorial Day weekend, don't miss this event. It

contains a range of activities and, of course, lots of wonderful crab.

These events and festivals give a peek into Alaska's rich culture and customs. Don't miss the opportunity to party like a native and make unforgettable memories throughout your vacation.

A Good Laugh: Comedy Clubs and Theaters

Alaska may not be the first destination that springs to mind for comedy, but it boasts a strong comedy culture and venues where you can have a good laugh. Here are some noteworthy comedy clubs and theaters in the state:

1. Chilkat Facility for the Arts (Haines): While largely a performing arts facility, the Chilkat Center sometimes presents comedy events and stand-up artists, delivering a unique entertainment experience in the picturesque town of Haines.

2. Koot's (Anchorage): This bustling Anchorage business is noted for its numerous entertainment offerings, including live music, karaoke, and stand-up comedy evenings. It's a terrific spot to appreciate local and visiting comedians.

3. **4th Avenue Theatre (Anchorage):** This old theater periodically offers comedy acts and other entertainment. Check the schedule during your stay for a chance to witness a comedy show in a beautifully refurbished theater.

4. **The Marlin (Fairbanks):** The Marlin provides a combination of live music, open mic nights, and comedy acts. It's a popular venue for residents and tourists seeking some laughs and entertainment.

5. **Kootz Rootz (Girdwood):** Located inside the picturesque Girdwood neighborhood, Kootz Rootz periodically organizes comedy events in addition to its regular live acts. It's a relaxing area to enjoy some laughter.

6. **Myrna Loy Center (Helena):** This community center and theater conducts numerous activities, including

comedy acts. It's a cultural center where you may mingle with local artists and entertainers.

7. Fairview Inn (Talkeetna): This historic inn in Talkeetna typically includes live music and comedy performances. Enjoy a night of hilarity in this lovely Alaskan village.

8. Bear's Tooth Tavern (Anchorage): While mostly a popular pizza tavern and theater, Bear's Tooth sometimes organizes comedy nights. Enjoy amazing meals and a nice laugh in a relaxed atmosphere.

Keep in mind that Alaska's comedy culture may not be as broad as in larger places, but it provides a distinct and personal experience. Check local event listings and venues for forthcoming comedy acts during your vacation to the Last Frontier.

Dining Adventures Beyond Compare

Alaska boasts a rich culinary scene that extends beyond its wilderness image. While you may experience fresh seafood, you'll also discover a selection of exotic cuisines.

1. Seafood Sensations: Alaska is known for its seafood. Enjoy fresh catches including wild salmon, halibut, king crab, and more. For a genuine Alaskan experience, try a seafood boil or feast at a crab shack by the shore.

2. Wild Game Delights: Game meat connoisseurs may taste meals like reindeer, moose, and even bear meat. These unusual tastes are best explored at local restaurants that specialize in game food.

3. Foraged Feasts: Discover the world of foraged meals, where you may taste wild berries, mushrooms, and other delicacies. Many Alaskan restaurants include these elements in their cuisine, delivering a taste of the region's natural richness.

4. Native Alaskan Cuisine: Explore the distinctive tastes of Alaska by sampling meals steeped in Native Alaskan customs. Look for eateries that sell meals like fried bread, salmon candy, and akutaq (Eskimo ice cream).

5. Craft Breweries and Distilleries: Alaska features a thriving craft beer and spirits sector. Sample local beers, from IPAs to stouts, at the state's breweries. Additionally, experience Alaskan-made vodka, gin, and other spirits at the expanding number of distilleries.

6. Fusion and International Influences: Alaska's varied population has brought worldwide culinary influences to the state. Enjoy fusion restaurants that mix numerous ethnic cuisines, from Asian fusion to Mexican-inspired food.

7. Fine Dining: For an elite experience, Alaska boasts fine dining restaurants providing gourmet tasting menus and wine pairings. These restaurants frequently offer locally produced foods and give a refined dining experience.

8. Alaskan Bakeries and Cafes: Don't forget to visit local bakeries and cafes for fresh pastries, artisan bread, and a cup of locally roasted coffee. It's a great way to start your day or indulge in a sweet treat.

9. Food Trucks & Street Eats: Alaska's food truck sector has been slowly increasing, delivering fast, excellent meals for people on the move. Look for food trucks providing anything from gourmet burgers to unique foreign delicacies.

10. Local Food Festivals: If your visit overlaps with one of Alaska's food festivals, don't miss the opportunity to indulge in a vast assortment of foods produced by local chefs and craftsmen.

The Alaskan culinary scene is an interesting trip for food connoisseurs. Whether you're a seafood lover, an experimental eater, or someone seeking exotic cuisines, Alaska offers something to suit every pallet. Be sure to investigate local suggestions and seek out unique eating experiences throughout your vacation.

Craft Breweries and Pubs

Alaska's craft brewery and pub sector has been slowly increasing, delivering a broad assortment of native tastes and distinctive beers. Whether you're a beer connoisseur or simply want to unwind in a quiet atmosphere, you'll find a warm welcome at Alaskan breweries and pubs.

1. Local Craft Beers: Alaska's craft brewers pride themselves on crafting distinctive, small-batch beers. You may try a broad array of beer varieties, from hoppy IPAs to deep stouts, frequently created with locally produced ingredients.

2. Tasting Rooms: Many breweries feature tasting rooms where you may try a flight of their beers. This is a terrific way to find your favorite Alaskan beers. Make it a point to the staff for ideas.

3. stunning Locations: Several breweries are located in gorgeous surroundings, affording stunning views of the surrounding landscape. Enjoy your drink on an outside terrace with breathtaking panoramas or cuddle up inside by the fireplace during the colder months.

4. **Local Flavors:** Some brewers add Alaskan elements into their beverages, such as wild berries, spruce needles, and even glacier water. These unusual tastes represent the local terroir and provide an authentic experience of Alaska.

5. **Brewery Tours:** whether you're interested in the beer-making process, check whether the brewery gives tours. You may learn about the brewing techniques, the importance of the ingredients, and the history of the brewery.

6. **Pub Fare:** Many breweries have connected pubs that offer wonderful cuisine, including meals meant to mix nicely with their brews. Enjoy favorites including burgers, fish & chips, and substantial sandwiches.

7. **Local Hangouts:** Brewpubs commonly serve as local hangout locations, so you'll get a sense of Alaskan

culture and friendliness. Strike up talks with welcoming locals and other visitors while drinking your beer.

8. Craft Beer Events: If your visit overlaps with a local craft beer event, consider participating. These events generally include live music, food trucks, and a large range of craft beers from different brewers.

9. Family-Friendly Atmosphere: Many brewpubs accept families, so you can relax with a drink while the kids enjoy a meal. Some even feature activities or outdoor places for youngsters.

10. Souvenirs: Don't forget to check whether the brewery has items available for purchase. You could discover T-shirts, glasses, or other keepsakes to recall your stay.

Exploring Alaska's craft brewery and pub scene is a fascinating opportunity to immerse yourself in the local culture, meet with friendly Alaskans, and savor the unique flavors the area has to offer. Whether you're an experienced beer enthusiast or simply someone wanting to relax in a nice setting, you're likely to find something to tickle your palette.

Hangout Spots Loved by Locals

When it comes to hangout areas adored by residents in Alaska, you're in for a treat. Alaskans have a profound respect for their unique environment, and their favorite sites typically reflect this passion for nature, culture, and community. Here are several hangout locations where you may enjoy the warmth of Alaskan hospitality:

1. **Coffee Shops with Character:** Alaska enjoys a strong coffee culture, with pleasant coffee shops sprinkled throughout its communities. These areas act as centers for folks to meet, speak, and enjoy a warm beverage. Be prepared for friendly baristas and coffee lovers who take their brews seriously. Try a cup of locally roasted coffee and participate in discussions with regulars.

2. **Trailhead Gathering:** Many Alaskans are outdoor enthusiasts, and trailheads frequently serve as unofficial

gathering sites. Whether it's for a stroll, a cross-country ski trip, or a leisurely walk, people commonly assemble at the beginning sites of their favorite paths. You'll discover a feeling of camaraderie and a common enthusiasm for the outdoors.

3. Brewpubs & Craft Beer Bars: The craft beer culture in Alaska is thriving, and brewpubs are more than simply locations to get a drink; they are social hubs. With an engaging environment, wonderful cuisine, and a choice of locally-made beers, these locations pull in both locals and tourists. Strike up talks with locals over a pint or flight of artisan beer.

4. Local Eateries: Alaska is famed for its seafood, and people have their favorite seafood shacks and eateries. These eateries frequently serve fresh catches of the day, providing anything from salmon to king crab. It's a fantastic chance to enjoy Alaskan seafood and learn about the state's culinary heritage.

5. Community activities: Keep an eye out for local activities, such as farmers' markets, cultural festivals, and concerts. These meetings give a genuine peek into Alaskan life and provide a chance to engage with locals who are proud to share their history.

6. **bookshops and Libraries:** Alaska's independent bookshops and public libraries are more than simply places to read; they are community hubs. Engage in talks about Alaskan literature, history, and culture with friendly residents who are enthusiastic about their state.

7. **Art Galleries and Studios:** The art scene in Alaska is booming, and many artists offer their studios to the public. Explore art galleries and studios to meet local artists, view their works, and perhaps buy unique items to take home as mementos.

8. **beautiful Overlooks:** Alaska's stunning landscapes provide several beautiful overlooks and vistas. These sites give a chance to enjoy the awe-inspiring beauty of the state with other tourists and residents alike. Conversations frequently concentrate on the landscape and personal experiences in the woods.

9. Local Parks and Recreation Areas: Public parks and recreational places are vital to Alaskans' lives. Visit these regions to indulge in outdoor activities and meet residents who like hiking, bicycling, fishing, and picnics.

10. Community Centers: Alaska's community centers are sites for activities, from fitness courses to arts and crafts. Engage with locals while engaging in activities that interest you.

When you visit these hangout locations, you'll immediately find that Alaskans are a kind and sociable lot, keen to share their excitement for their state. Don't be shocked if you leave these sites with new friends and a stronger appreciation of Alaska's distinctive culture.

Chapter 8: Exploring the Beauty of National Parks

Explore Alaska's National Parks for beautiful wilderness excursions. Denali has North America's highest mountain, while Glacier Bay provides marine marvels. Hike beside glaciers in Kenai Fjords, or discover seclusion in Wrangell-St. Elias, the biggest U.S. national park. Witness brown bears in Katmai, and embrace the lonely environment in Gates of the Arctic. Explore dunes in Kobuk Valley. These parks offer amazing vistas, outdoor activities, and animal encounters.

Kenai Fjords National Park and Preserve

Nestled in the rocky wilderness of Alaska's Kenai Peninsula, Kenai Fjords National Park and Preserve is a destination of awe-inspiring beauty and unspoiled natural treasures. Covering over 1,000 square miles, the park is recognized for its magnificent fjords, tidewater glaciers, and plentiful wildlife.

1. The Fjords and Glaciers: At the core of the park's attractiveness are its beautiful fjords, sculpted by the retreat of glaciers over millennia. The deep, narrow inlets are flanked by high rocks and stunning surroundings. Visitors may experience the stunning spectacle of tidewater glaciers, such as Aialik Glacier and Holgate Glacier, calving into the freezing seas with loud booms.

2. Wildlife Abundance: Kenai Fjords is a refuge for wildlife aficionados. The frigid seas teem with marine life, including humpback whales, orcas, sea otters, harbor seals, and sea lions. Birdwatchers will be charmed by the park's numerous bird populations, such as puffins, cormorants, and bald eagles. On land, tourists may observe brown bears, moose, and mountain goats.

3. Cruising and Kayaking: One of the greatest ways to experience the park's fjords is by joining a boat trip or kayaking excursion. These expeditions give a close-up glimpse of the glaciers, animals, and craggy coastline.

Many cruises leave from the adjacent town of Seward, offering a gateway to the park's aquatic delights.

4. **Harding Icefield:** At the heart of Kenai Fjords lies the huge Harding Icefield, the source of countless glaciers that flow down to the sea. Visitors may go on a hard climb to Exit Glacier, which affords awe-inspiring vistas of the icefield. It's a monument to the huge forces driving this environment.

5. **Ranger Programs:** The park's rangers provide instructive programs, including guided walks and discussions. These programs give insights into the park's geology, glaciology, and the flora and animals that call it home.

6. **Cultural Connections:** Kenai Fjords have cultural importance for the indigenous Alutiiq and Dena'ina people, who have resided in the area for thousands of years. Learning about their customs and history adds dimension to the visiting experience.

7. Hiking paths: The park has various hiking paths, each presenting a distinct view of the scenery. The lengthier, more strenuous treks lead to excellent vistas and the potential to observe animals.

8. Conservation and study: Kenai Fjords is not just a location of natural beauty but also a hotspot for scientific study. It's a vital location for investigating climate change, glacier dynamics, and ecosystem health. Understanding these changes is crucial for the park's preservation.

9. Exit Glacier Nature Center: Located near Seward, the Exit Glacier Nature Center is a visitor center providing exhibits and information on the park's natural and cultural heritage. It's a wonderful starting place for your excursion into Kenai Fjords.

Visiting Kenai Fjords National Park and Preserve is a voyage into a pristine environment where the beauty of nature reigns supreme. Whether you're exploring the chilly fjords, experiencing glaciers in action, or viewing the rich species, this park delivers an experience that leaves an everlasting impact. It's a reminder of the great beauty and resilience of our natural environment.

The Grandeur of Glacier Bay National Park

Nestled in the secluded tundra of Southeast Alaska, Glacier Bay National Park and Preserve stands as a tribute to the raw, unadulterated grandeur of nature. Covering over 3.3 million acres, this enormous park is famed for its breathtaking scenery, diversified animals, and the ever-changing drama of its glaciers. It's a location where the powers of nature take center stage, and tourists are treated to a once-in-a-lifetime experience.

1. **Dynamic Glacial Landscape:** The park's most noticeable feature is the awe-inspiring tidewater glaciers. These huge rivers of ice, including Margerie Glacier and Grand Pacific Glacier, span from mountaintops down to the sea. Visitors may experience the thundering sight of glaciers calving when large pieces of ice break free and fall into the bay's icy waters.

2. Rich Biodiversity: Glacier Bay features a stunning assortment of species. Humpback whales, orcas, sea otters, and seals frequent the bay's waters. On land, brown bears, moose, and mountain goats wander the lush woods and steep terrain. Birdwatchers will be amazed by the rich wildlife, including bald eagles and puffins.

3. Spectacular Fjords: The bay is bordered by steep, rocky fjords sculpted by receding glaciers. These deep, narrow inlets form a dramatic background for exploration, and kayaking is a popular method to get up close to the fjords' towering cliffs and tranquil bays.

4. Cultural Significance: The park has profound cultural links to the Tlingit people, who have occupied the area for generations. The park's rangers and interpreters share insights into the Tlingit's history, customs, and strong connection to this area.

5. Adventurous Activities: Glacier Bay provides numerous outdoor activities for guests to immerse themselves in this beautiful area. Hiking, camping, fishing, and boating are popular alternatives. The West

Arm and Bartlett Cove sections are good settings for exploring the park.

6. Scientific Interest: Beyond its scenic attractiveness, Glacier Bay is a living laboratory for scientists investigating glaciology and ecological succession. The retreat of glaciers has uncovered desolate areas, which have progressively been recovered by plant life. This gives a unique chance to investigate natural ecological processes.

7. Conservation Efforts: Glacier Bay National Park and Preserve is devoted to protecting this unique habitat. It's a vital location for continuing climate change research, enabling scientists to examine the consequences of glacier retreat and altering ecosystems.

8. Visitor facilities: The park's visitor facilities, notably the Glacier Bay Visitor Center at Bartlett Cove, offer educational resources, maps, and ranger-led programs to assist visitors in better understanding and appreciating this unique area.

Glacier Bay National Park and Preserve provides a dramatic voyage into a realm of ice, water, and a pristine environment. Whether you're here to see the glaciers' majesty, meet its rich animals, or immerse yourself in its calm fjords, this park guarantees an experience that lingers long after you've gone. It's a site where the great force of nature is on full display, reminding us of the beauty and fragility of our world.

A Journey into Wrangell-St. Elias National Park

Wrangell-St. Elias National Park and Preserve, situated in southern Alaska, is a place of superlatives. As the biggest national park in the United States, it offers amazing variety and vastness, encompassing an area greater than the country of Switzerland. Here, you'll discover a panorama that appears to have no boundaries, boasting gigantic mountains, massive glaciers, and pure nature.

The park's highlight is the Wrangell Mountains, a range that comprises some of the highest peaks in North

America. Among them is Mount St. Elias, the second-highest summit in the United States. These mountains are a magnet for mountaineers and adventure seekers eager to accomplish some of the most arduous climbs in the world.

Glaciers are another characteristic aspect of this park. The Bagley Icefield, one of the biggest non-polar icefields worldwide, gives rise to many glaciers that flow through the valleys. The sight of glaciers meeting temperate rainforests is a unique and spectacular encounter.

Visitors to Wrangell-St. Elias may indulge in many outdoor activities, such as hiking, trekking, canoeing, and even flightseeing trips that give aerial views of this immense wilderness. The park is also home to various species, including grizzly bears, wolves, and eagles.

With minimal infrastructure, it remains a real wilderness getaway. Whether you're an explorer, a nature lover, or someone seeking isolation in a distant and undisturbed terrain, Wrangell-St. Elias National Park provides an amazing trek into the heart of Alaska's untamed environment.

Protecting Arctic Wilderness: ANWR

The Arctic National Wildlife Refuge (ANWR) is a pristine and environmentally critical territory situated in the northeastern section of Alaska. Covering over 19 million acres, ANWR is one of the few wild areas on Earth, and it's recognized for its unspoiled wildness, unique ecosystems, and critical role in conserving the natural environment.

ANWR is a location of superlatives. It's home to one of the biggest and most intact ecosystems in the world, containing arctic tundra, mountains, rivers, and coastal plains. The refuge is also home to an astonishing diversity of wildlife, including iconic animals like polar bears, caribou, muskoxen, and a profusion of bird species. These species depend on ANWR for breeding, eating, and refuge.

One of the most well-known portions of ANWR is the coastal plain, sometimes referred to as the "1002 Area." This region has been a focal focus of conservation efforts and controversies for many years because of its great biological value. It serves as a calving habitat for the Porcupine Caribou Herd, a crucial component of the region's environment.

Beyond its biological value, ANWR offers cultural significance for Alaska Natives, who have depended on this area for thousands of years. Protecting ANWR is not simply a conservation priority but also an acknowledgment of the Indigenous peoples who have stewarded this territory for decades.

Efforts to safeguard ANWR have been continuing, including designating areas of it as wilderness to ensure its continued pristine nature. ANWR is a symbol of our commitment to conserving the world's remaining great wild areas for future generations.

Visitors to ANWR may discover its pristine landscapes via guided tours, backpacking expeditions, and photographic excursions. While many sites are isolated and tough to get, they provide a unique chance to enjoy the raw splendor of the Arctic.

Conservation and maintenance of the Arctic National Wildlife Refuge are crucial. It is a tribute to our determination to safeguard Earth's last wild and untamed regions, ensuring they remain a haven for animals, the environment, and generations to come.

The Majesty of Tongass National Forest

The Tongass National Forest, frequently referred to as the "crown jewel" of the United States' national forest system, is a stunning and untouched wilderness situated in Southeast Alaska. Spanning roughly 16.7 million acres, it is not just the biggest national forest but one of the largest temperate rainforests in the world. The Tongass is a site of breathtaking vistas, complex ecosystems, and unrivaled natural beauty.

1. Lush Rainforests: The Tongass is recognized for its lush and colorful rainforests, marked by towering Sitka spruce and western red cedar trees, green mosses, and a multitude of plant life. The forest gets considerable quantities of rain, with annual precipitation frequently topping 100 inches in certain regions.

2. **spectacular Scenery:** Visitors to the Tongass are treated to spectacular panoramas of fjords, glaciers, mountains, and islands. It's a paradise for outdoor lovers, giving chances for hiking, camping, boating, and animal watching. Misty Fjords National Monument, a component of the Tongass, is especially noted for its awe-inspiring scenery.

3. **Abundant animals:** The Tongass provides a home for a surprising diversity of animals, including black and brown bears, wolves, deer, bald eagles, and innumerable types of fish. The seas around the forest are rich with salmon and other marine life, making it a crucial location for conservation.

4. **Cultural Significance:** The Tongass is rich in cultural heritage, and it's home to numerous Native Alaskan towns. Indigenous peoples have lived in peace with this

land for thousands of years, living on its resources and handing down their cultural history.

5. Outdoor Recreation: The forest provides several recreational options, such as hiking, fishing, kayaking, and wildlife photography. There are miles of trails, camping, and cottages for those who prefer to immerse themselves in this natural treasure.

6. Conservation and Sustainability: Efforts are in place to safeguard the Tongass and guarantee sustainable land management. Conservation projects strive to conserve the forest's natural nature, while sustainable logging techniques contribute to local economies and wood sectors.

7. Tourism and Education: The Tongass welcomes tourists from throughout the globe. Tour operators and interpretive centers give educational opportunities about the forest's environmental and cultural value.

The Tongass National Forest offers the essence of untamed natural beauty, where unspoiled wilderness meets biological variety. Preserving this spectacular terrain is crucial not just for conservation but also for future generations to explore, enjoy, and comprehend the value of these wild areas on our planet. It is a tribute to the dedication to safeguarding our planet's most magnificent natural assets.

Chapter 9: Savoring Alaskan Delicacies

Experience the variety and exquisite cuisine of Alaska. Dive into seafood specialties, from fresh salmon to luscious king crab legs. Savor wild game like moose and caribou, individually cooked to perfection. Explore foraged foods that embody the spirit of the wild, including berries and more. Immerse yourself in Native Alaskan cuisine, a fascinating tapestry of traditions and tastes. And don't forget to enjoy the offerings from craft brewers and distilleries, merging the finest of local and foreign inspirations into a gastronomic trip like no other.

Feast on Fresh Seafood Delights

Indulge in the wealth of the Alaskan seas as you feast on fresh seafood delicacies. Alaska is known for its world-class seafood, and your taste buds are in for a treat. Try delicious wild salmon, famous for its rich taste and Omega-3 goodness. Savor the delicate, soft flesh of king crab legs, a genuine delicacy. Dive into halibut, recognized for its gentle flavor and flaky texture. Don't miss the opportunity to savor the freshest shrimp, scallops, and a variety of shellfish. Whether you want it grilled, roasted, or pan-seared, the seafood in Alaska is a gourmet experience waiting to be discovered.

Wild Game Adventures on Your Plate

In Alaska, wild game isn't simply a supper; it's a cultural experience. The state provides a selection of unusual and tasty game meats that will thrill any cuisine connoisseur. Elk, caribou, moose, and reindeer give lean, rich slices suitable for grilling, roasting, or stewing. You may experience the powerful flavor of bear meat, a typical Alaskan option. And let's not forget the soft and delectable wild boar, typically served in varied culinary techniques.

With each meal, you're not only savoring the vast, rough environment of Alaska but also its history and heritage. These wild animal meats give a real flavor of the outdoors and are a must-try for adventurous foodies searching for a distinctly Alaskan gastronomic experience.

Nature's Pantry: Foraged Foods

Foraging in Alaska is a gourmet excursion like no other. This zone of enormous wildness provides a wealth of food plants, mushrooms, and other natural treasures waiting to be found. Some foraged foods you'll encounter in Alaska include:

1. **Wild Berries:** Blueberries, salmonberries, cloudberries, and cranberries are just a few of the delightful berries you could uncover on your foraging adventure.

2. **Edible Plants:** Nettles, fireweed shoots, and fiddlehead ferns may be converted into wonderful recipes.

3. **Mushrooms:** Morel and porcini mushrooms are coveted discoveries for culinary connoisseurs.

4. **Wild Herbs:** Spruce tips, fireweed blooms, and seashore greens may offer unusual tastes to your cuisine.

Foraging in Alaska ties you to the earth in a meaningful manner, enabling you to experience the clean and untamed flavors of the Last Frontier. While foraging, remember to respect the ecosystem and gather ethically, only taking what you need.

Savoring Native Alaskan Cuisine

Native Alaskan cuisine is a tribute to the state's rich cultural legacy, where traditional dishes and cooking techniques continue to be appreciated. When experiencing Native Alaskan cuisine, you'll meet meals and ingredients like:

1. **Salmon:** A mainstay in the Alaskan diet, salmon comes in numerous kinds including king, sockeye, and coho. It's prepared by smoking, drying, or even consumed fresh.

2. **Muktuk:** This is whale fat and skin, a traditional Inuit cuisine, sometimes served frozen. It's a delicacy with a distinct texture and taste.

3. Akutaq: Also known as "Eskimo ice cream," akutaq is created with whipped fat (seal or moose), fruit, and occasionally fish. It's a sweet and savory pleasure.

4. Fry Bread: A favorite among many tribes, fry bread is deep-fried dough that may be served as a sweet treat or utilized in savory recipes.

5. Reindeer: Often found in delicacies like reindeer sausage, this meat is lean and rich in taste.

6. Boiled Seal: Prepared by cooking seal flesh or flippers until soft, it's a filling and healthy meal.

7. Wild Berries: Blueberries, cloudberries, and salmonberries are prevalent in desserts or relished fresh.

Savoring Native Alaskan food provides a unique gastronomic journey through the cultural traditions of indigenous people, demonstrating their strong connection to the land and its resources. When sampling these foods, it's not just about the flavor but also a chance to understand the history and legacy of Alaska's native populations.

Raising a Glass: Craft Breweries and Distilleries

Alaska's artisan brewers and distilleries are a tribute to the state's creativity and devotion to excellent drinks. When you visit these venues, you're in for a wonderful experience that goes beyond standard beer and spirits.

1. Craft Breweries: Alaska features a thriving craft beer sector. Breweries like Alaskan Brewing Company and Midnight Sun Brewing Company have achieved notoriety for their distinctive, regionally inspired beverages. Many of these brewers integrate Alaskan products, such as spruce tips and wild berries, generating tastes that encapsulate the character of the area.

2. Distilleries: The artisan distillery movement has taken root in Alaska, creating high-quality spirits with a distinct Alaskan touch. You may try locally created vodkas, gins, and even whiskies. Some distilleries employ local grains, while others experiment with uncommon additives, producing in unique and unforgettable tastes.

3. Tasting Rooms: Most brewers and distilleries provide tasting rooms, enabling you to try a range of drinks in a relaxing setting. It's a chance to interact with the brewers or distillers, hear about their methods, and receive insights into the art of making beer and spirits.

4. Touring and Events: Many craft brewers and distilleries arrange tours of their operations. These excursions provide an educational experience, providing light on the manufacturing techniques and the necessity of utilizing local foods. You could even discover live music, cuisine pairings, and events at these establishments, making them fantastic places to connect with residents and other tourists.

5. Unique Flavors: Alaska's artisan brewers and distilleries are recognized for pushing the limits of taste. You may anticipate anything from rich and strong stouts to refreshing and fruity ales. And when it comes to spirits, you'll discover distinctly Alaskan components integrated into their flavor characteristics.

Visiting these small breweries and distilleries is a fantastic way to immerse yourself in Alaska's local culture. It's an opportunity to engage with the community, admire their passion for the craft, and raise your glass to the unique tastes of the Last Frontier. Whether you're a beer fan, a spirit expert, or just someone seeking a good time, Alaska's craft beverage culture offers something for everyone.

International Flavors and Fusion

Alaskan cuisine is a rich tapestry of local resources, cultural influences, and culinary ingenuity. While the state has a rich legacy of natural dishes and wild animals, it also reflects foreign influences and fusion cuisine. Here's an overview of how Alaskan cuisine embraces foreign tastes and fusion:

1. Russian Influence: Alaska's history includes an era of Russian colonialism. This background is visible in meals like borscht, a robust beet soup, and piroshki, savory pastries stuffed with meats or vegetables. These

Russian-inspired meals are adored by Alaskans and tourists alike.

2. Asian Fusion: The influence of Asian cuisine may be evident in Alaskan delicacies such as salmon teriyaki and miso-marinated blackfish. The incorporation of soy, ginger, and other Asian spices adds depth and complexity to the tastes of Alaskan fish.

3. Scandinavian Flavors: Scandinavian immigrants have made their stamp on Alaskan cuisine. Iconic delicacies like lutefisk, a preserved fish dish, and lefse, a soft flatbread, may be found at local gatherings and celebrations. Alaskans have merged these Scandinavian characteristics with local ingredients, producing a unique mixture of tastes.

4. Mexican-Inspired Fare: Alaska's culinary culture has accepted the influence of Mexican cuisine, creating delicacies like salmon tacos and reindeer burritos. The mix of Alaskan fish and Mexican spices results in fresh and spicy tastes.

5. Pacific Rim Inspirations: Alaska's closeness to the Pacific Rim has led to the inclusion of items like seaweed, sushi, and teriyaki sauce into native meals. The mix of these coastal tastes lends an intriguing depth to Alaskan cuisine.

6. Native American Traditions: Alaskan Native cuisine is strongly embedded in the state's culinary culture. Indigenous people have handed down traditional recipes for centuries. Ingredients like wild game, fish, berries, and edible plants continue to be cherished, and some modern chefs combine these aspects into contemporary recipes, displaying respect for local culinary traditions.

7. Fusion Restaurants: Fusion restaurants in Alaska give a chance to explore unique mixes of foreign tastes. These cafes regularly integrate Alaskan products with varied culinary traditions, resulting in unique and tasty meals.

8. Culinary Events: Alaskan food festivals and events showcase the state's unique culinary influences. These events provide a diversity of ethnic cuisines and fusion meals, enabling you to experience anything from Asian-inspired seafood to Russian-influenced stews.

9. Homegrown Ingredients: The blend of foreign cuisines wouldn't be possible without Alaska's bountiful natural resources. From wild-caught salmon and halibut to foraged berries and mushrooms, local ingredients play a significant part in producing these distinct culinary experiences.

Alaska's cuisine is a monument to the state's unique history and the merging of civilizations over generations. Whether you're tasting Russian specialties, experiencing Asian-inspired seafood, or relishing Mexican-Alaskan fusion, the diverse tapestry of various cuisines in the Last Frontier guarantees a memorable gastronomic adventure.

Chapter 10: The Great Alaskan Road Trip

Embarking on an Alaskan road trip is an exciting experience through some of the most stunning scenery in the world. The Last Frontier is a vast and untamed wilderness, where roads and byways wind through towering mountains, virgin forests, and breathtaking coastline panoramas. A road journey here offers encounters with magnificent animals, calm lakes, and attractive tiny villages.

Begin in Anchorage, the state's biggest city, then take the road toward Denali National Park. The route takes you past the magnificent Matanuska Glacier, where picture stops are a must. In Denali, witness the magnificence of North America's highest mountain, Denali, once known as Mount McKinley.

From there, travel south via the Kenai Peninsula, a location of outdoor delights. The Kenai Fjords, with its ice fjords and marine life, will leave you in wonder. Keep a lookout for bald eagles, moose, and humpback whales. You may also go kayaking or sail past the towering glaciers.

Continue your Alaskan road adventure eastward into the ancient town of Valdez, hidden in the Chugach Mountains. Here, you may explore the Worthington Glacier and Prince William Sound's tranquil waters.

As you go back north towards Fairbanks, stop at the eccentric small town of Talkeetna and soak in the unique environment. Fairbanks provides unique activities, such as relaxing in natural hot springs and experiencing the Northern Lights throughout the winter months.

Alaska's highways also give access to distant wilderness regions. The trek down the unpaved Denali Highway is a perfect example. This dirt road gives you a chance to view animals and access hiking paths that feel like they're your own.

The Great Alaskan Road Trip is more than simply a drive; it's an experiential voyage through nature's magnificence. Be prepared for rough terrains, so gear your car adequately. Make overnight breaks in lovely cottages or campsites beneath a starlit sky. Immerse yourself in the splendor of Alaska's wilderness on this once-in-a-lifetime excursion by automobile.

Navigating Alaska's Roads

Exploring Alaska by road is an unrivaled journey, allowing access to the state's immense wilderness, stunning landscapes, and lovely communities. Navigating Alaska's roadways is a fascinating tour through some of the most spectacular and desolate landscapes in the United States.

1. Anchorage: The Gateway

Your Alaskan road journey often starts in Anchorage, the state's biggest city. Stock up on supplies and immerse yourself in the local culture. Anchorage is noted for its diversified food scene which gives a flavor of metropolitan Alaska.

2. Scenic Drives

Alaska's road network runs for hundreds of kilometers, including prominent roads like the Seward Highway, Glenn Highway, and Parks Highway. These routes allow access to magnificent vistas including Turnagain Arm, Matanuska Glacier, and Denali National Park.

3. Denali National Park

The crown gem of Alaska's interior is Denali National Park, home to North America's tallest mountain. The Parks Highway leads you there, and once within the park, access is confined to a shuttle bus system, enabling you to observe animals and explore nature.

4. Kenai Peninsula

Journeying south to the Kenai Peninsula is a necessity. Stop at destinations like Kenai Fjords National Park, where glaciers meet the ocean, and Homer, a lovely fishing town noted for its art and panoramic vistas.

5. Valdez and Wrangell-St. Elias

Head east towards Valdez, a town located in the Chugach Mountains. The trip from Valdez to the beautiful Wrangell-St. Elias National Park leads you beyond the Worthington Glacier and gives a picture of rural Alaskan living.

6. Talkeetna and the Denali Highway

The eccentric village of Talkeetna is a popular visit with its colorful buildings and unusual vibe. The Denali Highway, however hard for the faint of heart, rewards with breathtaking panoramas of the Alaska Range and possibilities for animal observation.

7. Fairbanks and Beyond

As you journey north towards Fairbanks, discover off-the-beaten-path sites, soak in natural hot springs, and enjoy the stunning Northern Lights.

8. Tips for the Road

Traveling Alaska's highways may be tough. Weather conditions, animal interactions, and the enormous distances between settlements need cautious preparation. Be sure your car is well-maintained, stock up on supplies, and know your route.

9. Camping and Accommodations

Alaska provides several campgrounds and cottages for guests. Embrace the spirit of adventure by camping beneath the midnight sun, but also have a list of lodgings as a backup.

10. Wildlife Encounters

Along the journey, keep a lookout for moose, bears, eagles, and more. Respect animals from a safe distance and observe Leave No Trace principles.

An Alaskan road trip is a journey into the heart of the Last Frontier, delivering unique experiences and a closer connection to the unspoiled landscape. Prepare for the journey of a lifetime as you drive Alaska's highways, where every turn unveils a new side of this beautiful state.

Explore the Kenai Peninsula

The Kenai Peninsula is a world-renowned treasure in Alaska, a site where breathtaking scenery, varied animals, and rich cultural experiences combine. This enthralling location is a playground for outdoor lovers, explorers, and anybody wanting to enjoy the untouched splendor of the Last Frontier.

An Introduction to the Kenai Peninsula

Nestled in southern Alaska, the Kenai Peninsula is a region of superlatives. It's where the continent's biggest national park, Wrangell-St. Elias meets the Gulf of Alaska's beautiful seas. Covering over 25,000 square miles, the peninsula has magnificent fjords, glaciers, and deep-blue lakes, making it a treasure trove of natural delights. Its proximity to Anchorage, along with a network of well-maintained highways, adds to its attraction.

Seward: Where Mountains Meet the Sea

Your trip onto the Kenai Peninsula frequently starts at Seward, a picturesque seaside town noted for its crucial role in Alaska's history. From here, the entrance to the spectacular Kenai Fjords National Park is effortless. Prepare for awe-inspiring boat cruises where you'll experience the drama of tidewater glaciers calving into the sea, along with intimate encounters with marine species including humpback whales, sea lions, and puffins.

Homer: Where Art Meets Nature

Homer, another seaside town, is a hotbed of creative expression and provides breathtaking landscapes of the Kachemak Bay. Visit the famed Pratt Museum to comprehend the area's rich history and art, and don't miss the chance to trek to Grace Ridge for breathtaking vistas.

Kenai and Soldotna: Angler's Paradise

For fisherman, the Kenai and Soldotna rivers are famed for their salmon runs. Try your luck at capturing a magnificent king salmon, and, if you come in July, you could watch the exhilarating sportfishing dip-netting on the Kenai River.

Cooper Landing: An Enclave of Serenity

For a calm vacation, travel to Cooper Landing, a tiny, lovely village located in the Chugach National Forest. Here, the Kenai River quietly meanders through an emerald valley, enticing you to fish or walk. Be sure to visit the Russian River Falls, a fantastic area for bear-watching.

National Parks: Rugged Adventures Await

The Kenai Peninsula provides a gateway to two remarkable national parks: Kenai Fjords National Park and Katmai National Park. The former provides marine and glacier beauty, while the latter is noted for its coastal brown bear population. Take a short trip to Katmai for an incredible bear-viewing adventure at Brooks Falls.

Outdoor Activities: The Peninsula's Playground:

In addition to fishing and animal encounters, the Kenai Peninsula is a playground for hikers, kayakers, and explorers of all sorts. Trails like the Resurrection Pass Trail give vistas into the heart of Alaskan nature, while chances for kayaking, rafting, and flightseeing are numerous.

Local Culture: Connections with Alaskan Life

Meet the friendly residents, enjoy their culture, and attend yearly events that embody the character of the peninsula. Visit the Kenai Visitor and Cultural Center to experience the area's indigenous history and modern creative manifestations.

Wrapping up Your Adventure

Leaving the Kenai Peninsula may not be simple. As you finish off your tour, consider the Alaska Wildlife Conservation Center near Portage, a facility committed to protecting Alaskan wildlife. And with a feeling of amazement and a plethora of memories, return to Anchorage or go on your next Alaskan trip.

The Kenai Peninsula is a microcosm of Alaska's awe-inspiring majesty, where nature reigns supreme, and any outdoor enthusiast's dream may come true. The appeal of this unspoiled area beckons you to explore its different landscapes, enjoy its rich culture, and interact with its wonderful animals. It's a bit of Alaska's wild heart that will forever remain with you.

Discover the Wilderness of Denali National Park

Denali National Park, a massive expanse of untouched wilderness tucked in the heart of Alaska, epitomizes the spirit of the Last Frontier like no other location. Home to North America's tallest mountain, Denali, this renowned park offers a trip into the heart of Alaska's natural treasures and untamed landscapes.

An Introduction to Denali National Park

The Denali National Park and Preserve, comprising over 6 million acres, is a huge, pristine playground for environment enthusiasts, hikers, and animal watchers. Located roughly 240 miles north of Anchorage, it's a land of superlatives, where the wilderness flourishes in all its splendor.

The Crown Jewel: Denali Peak

Denali, originally known as Mount McKinley, is the park's showpiece. Rising 20,310 feet above sea level, it's North America's highest peak and one of the world's most recognizable mountains. The name "Denali" means "the High One" in the original Athabascan language, an excellent description of this beautiful peak.

Wildlife Encounters: Nature's Abundance

Denali National Park is noted for its rich fauna. Grizzly bears, moose, wolves, caribou, Dall sheep, and golden eagles make this immense wilderness home. The park's protected status enables these critters to wander freely, presenting an exceptional opportunity for wildlife lovers and photographers.

The Denali Park Road: The Gateway to Adventure

The Denali Park Road, running 92 kilometers inside the park, is the principal route for seeing its attractions.

Private cars are only permitted on the first 15 kilometers; after that, visitors must employ the park's shuttle bus system, which allows an opportunity to dig further into the park's untamed heart.

Hiking and Backpacking: A Wild Playground
Denali National Park has a large network of paths that range in complexity. From shorter hikes ideal for all tourists to more strenuous wilderness hiking excursions, it appeals to explorers of every ability. The fresh, clear air, vast panoramas, and beautiful alpine landscape combine for an amazing hiking experience.

Ranger-Led Programs: Expert Guidance
Ranger-led events give an educational dimension to your stay. These skilled guides share insights into the park's natural history, geology, and fauna, boosting your enjoyment of this environment.

Alpenglow: A Visual Feast
The phenomenon known as alpenglow, when the snow-capped peaks become pink and yellow in the light

of the setting sun, is a strange vision in Denali. Be careful to photograph this amazing sight

.

Photography Paradise: Picture-Perfect Moments

Whether you're an amateur shutterbug or a seasoned photographer, Denali National Park is a wonderful setting. The dramatic landscapes, wide tundras, and diverse fauna give limitless opportunities for great images.

Wilderness Camping: A Unique Experience

Camping inside the park, among the woods, is an amazing experience. The park's approved campsites and backcountry permits offer a real interaction with the wild environment of Denali.

Local Culture: Connecting with the Athabascans

While touring the park, consider a visit to the Denali Visitor Center, where you may learn about the Athabascan aboriginal culture and its strong connection to this area. The art, storytelling, and customs of this indigenous tribe give a greater knowledge of Denali's past.

Closing Thoughts

Denali National Park serves as an untamed testimony to Alaska's raw splendor. It's a location of great proportions and natural wonders, where Denali's towering presence is matched only by the vibrant ecosystems it contains. Exploring this park is a voyage into the heart of Alaska's wildness, and every minute spent here is a memory carved in the spirit.

Experience the Magic of Fairbanks

Fairbanks, commonly nicknamed the "Golden Heart City," is a site where the charm of Alaska comes alive. Nestled in the state's interior, this thriving city provides a real Alaskan experience that's rich in history, culture, and natural beauty.

A Glimpse into Fairbanks

Fairbanks acts as a gateway to the Alaskan wilderness. It's not just the state's second-largest metropolis but also a flourishing town with a unique combination of modernity and history. This city epitomizes the essence of Alaska, providing a choice of excursions and experiences.

Northern Lights: Fairbanks' Celestial Spectacle

One of Fairbanks' most recognized attractions is its location beneath the "Aurora Oval," making it one of the finest sites for watching the Northern Lights, a heavenly dance of brilliant lights that adorn the night sky. Chase the auroras on guided tours, or just wander out on a clear winter night for a stunning show.

Pioneer Park: A Step Back in Time

For a taste of Alaskan history, Pioneer Park is a must-visit. This park re-creates an early 20th-century Alaskan hamlet, looking into the Gold Rush period. Explore museums, ride an antique riverboat, and have a sensation of going back in time.

The Gold Rush Legacy

Fairbanks' history is intricately entwined with the Gold Rush period, and you may learn about it at the University of Alaska Museum of the North. Discover the tales of intrepid prospectors and the gems they sought in this intriguing museum.

Chena Hot Springs: A Soak in Paradise

Not far from Fairbanks, you'll discover Chena Hot Springs, a year-round resort noted for its warm, relaxing waters. Soaking in these natural mineral springs surrounded by snow and ice is a classic Alaskan experience.

Arctic Wildlife: Natural Encounters

If you're a wildlife enthusiast, a visit to the Creamer's Field Migratory Waterfowl Refuge is a must. It's a refuge for migrating birds and a wonderful site for birding.

University of Alaska Fairbanks: Intellectual Hub:

The city is home to the University of Alaska Fairbanks, an intellectual hub of research and education. Consider wandering the campus, visiting museums, or attending public lectures and activities

.

Iditarod Trail Sled Dog Race: A Legendary Event
Fairbanks is a vital site for the renowned Iditarod Trail Sled Dog Race, known as "The Last Great Race." If you're traveling in March, you may watch the start or conclusion of this legendary event.

Unique Experiences
In Fairbanks, you may enjoy activities that are distinctly Alaskan, such as ice sculpture, ice fishing, and snowmobiling. These winter experiences allow you to immerse yourself in the true Alaskan way of life.

Cultural Encounters: Meeting the Locals
Fairbanks also gives insight into native cultures. You may engage with the Athabascan people, and the region's indigenous residents, and learn about their customs, artwork, and way of life.

Wrap-up: A City with a Heart of Gold

Fairbanks is a city that lives up to its moniker as the "Golden Heart." It provides a warm welcome, a strong connection to its past, and a gateway to the untamed grandeur of Alaska's interior. Your stay at Fairbanks will show a unique combination of urban activity and natural magnificence, creating a memorable chapter in your Alaskan experience.

Off-the-Beaten-Path Adventures

Alaska's charm doesn't simply lay in its well-known tourist spots; it's also about the unknown territory, secluded hideaways, and hidden treasures that offer unique and memorable experiences. Here, we'll look into some of Alaska's off-the-beaten-path excursions, allowing a chance to explore the Last Frontier in a manner few ever do.

1. Hiking the Crow Pass Trail

Situated near Girdwood, the Crow Pass Trail provides a fantastic backcountry trekking adventure. This path runs through deep woods, via glacier-fed rivers, and concludes with a historic hand tram crossing of the glacial river. It's a wonderful day trek for people seeking tranquility and natural beauty.

2. The Magic of McCarthy-Kennicott

Venture far into Wrangell-St. Elias National Park to find McCarthy and Kennicott. This neighborhood, once a thriving copper mining center, now seems like a well-preserved ghost town. Explore abandoned houses and go to the adjacent glaciers for a unique voyage back in time.

3. Anan Wildlife Observatory

Tucked deep in the Tongass National Forest, the Anan Wildlife Observatory gives a chance for a close encounter with black and brown bears. Witness salmon flows and bears in their natural environment. The property is accessible only by boat, adding to its hidden beauty.

4. Baird Glacier

For an exceptional journey, come to Baird Glacier in southeast Alaska. This involves a plane flight to reach this distant glacier, where you may explore ice caves, stroll through the beautiful environment, and experience the genuine seclusion that Alaska provides.

5. The Iditarod Trail

The legendary Iditarod Trail is more than simply a dog sled race; it's also a fantastic trekking trail. Embark on this historical road from Knik to Seward, and encounter wilderness, rivers, and breathtaking scenery. Along the journey, you'll witness rustic cottages and animals.

6. The Legend of Manley Hot Springs

Hidden deep inside the Yukon River Valley, Manley Hot Springs provides leisure in natural hot springs in a stunning environment. Stay at the lovely Manley Roadhouse, noted for its unique, friendly environment.

7. Kayaking at Glacier Bay

While Glacier Bay National Park isn't off-the-beaten-path in itself, kayaking across it is a unique opportunity to appreciate its magnificence. Paddle gently around the bay's tranquil waters and get up close to towering glaciers and aquatic life.

8. Wiseman and the Arctic Circle

Explore the tiny, historic village of Wiseman, where a few individuals live year-round amid the Brooks Range. Continue your adventure to reach the Arctic Circle, a legendary feat that few can claim.

9. Arctic National Wildlife Refuge

For the truly wilderness aficionados, the Arctic National Wildlife Refuge is a pristine expanse of untamed splendor. Fly into this isolated location for unequaled animal encounters, bird gazing, and the opportunity to explore the untamed Arctic scenery.

10. The End of the Road in Nome

Nome is Alaska's ultimate frontier. This secluded seaside town is famed for its gold rush past, and it remains a distinctive and somewhat lonely resort. Explore its ancient structures, or try your hand at gold panning.

While these activities are off the usual route, they demand careful preparation, self-sufficiency, and respect for the environment. When discovering these hidden jewels, you're guaranteed to have great experiences and feel the untamed heart of Alaska.

Connect with Alaskan Locals

Alaska is more than simply its breathtaking scenery; it's a place of tenacious and hospitable people, each having a story to tell and a piece of their culture to contribute. To properly enjoy the Last Frontier, engaging with locals is crucial. Here, we'll look into several methods to interact with Alaskans and develop a greater knowledge of this unique area.

1. Cultural Immersion

One of the most rewarding ways to interact with Alaskans is via cultural encounters. Visit local museums, art galleries, and cultural centers to learn about Alaska's indigenous people. In Anchorage, the Alaska Native Heritage Center gives insights into the state's numerous native traditions. Similarly, Fairbanks' Morris Thompson Cultural and Visitors Center gives an educational experience on the region's history.

2. Attend Local Festivals

Alaska has several festivals and events throughout the year, commemorating its history, arts, and customs. Events like the World Eskimo-Indian Olympics in Fairbanks and the Alaska State Fair in Palmer give a chance to meet with inhabitants and join in their celebrations.

3. Dine at Local Eateries

Alaskan cuisine is a reflection of the state's distinctive culture, integrating local ingredients with foreign influences. Opt for local cafés and street sellers to sample indigenous cuisines like salmon, moose, and bison. This isn't just about food; it's an opportunity to speak with restaurant owners and other diners, exchanging tales and laughing.

4. Attend Community Events

Keep an eye out for community activities, such as farmer's markets, artisan fairs, and town hall meetings. Engaging with locals in these contexts frequently leads to spontaneous relationships and honest interactions.

5. Join Local Tours

When visiting areas like Homer, Seward, or Talkeetna, consider taking tours conducted by expert guides who are frequently natives themselves. They share their affection for their hometowns and local mythology, offering you an insider's view.

6. Participate in Volunteer Activities

If you have any additional time during your stay, volunteer with local groups. Helping with community initiatives or conservation efforts not only links you with people but also enables you to give back to the areas that welcome you.

7. Explore Small Towns

The little settlements spread throughout Alaska are a treasure mine of authenticity. Places like Talkeetna, famed for its unique character, or McCarthy, a vestige of Alaska's copper mining heritage, give a look into ordinary life in the state.

8. Visit Native Villages

For a meaningful connection with Alaska's indigenous traditions, arrange a visit to native settlements. Learn about their customs, art, and way of life. Some trips, like those to the Inupiat community of Barrow or the Athabascan village of Ruby, provide an immersive experience.

9. Attend Native Dance Performances

Throughout Alaska, you may watch native dance performances, where storytelling, music, and dances are presented. These meetings allow appreciation of the rich traditions of Alaskan indigenous tribes.

10. Engage in Outdoor Activities

Whether fishing, hiking, or dog sledding, Alaska's outdoor activities generally include local guides who are enthusiastic about their land. These guides not only deliver amazing activities but also share their expertise and affection for the place.

When you engage with Alaskan residents, you'll get a more deep respect for the Last Frontier. Their tales, kindness, and love for their home will enhance your tour, making it a remarkable exploration of not just the state's natural treasures but also its beating heart: its people.

Chapter 11: A 7-Day Itinerary Vacation Plan to Alaska

Alaska's breadth and variety make it a great location for a week-long tour. This itinerary will take you to some of the state's most famous and stunning areas, delivering a view of its spectacular scenery, animals, and culture.

Day 1: Anchorage Arrival

Morning: Arrive in Anchorage, Alaska's biggest city, and settle into your lodgings.

Afternoon: Explore downtown Anchorage, where you'll discover museums, shopping, and restaurants. Don't miss the Anchorage Museum and the Alaska Native Heritage Center for an introduction to the state's culture.

Evening: Dine at a local restaurant, relishing fresh fish or traditional Alaskan meals.

Day 2: Denali National Park

Morning: Drive north to Denali National Park. The ride alone is a visual feast, with chances to observe animals like moose and Dall sheep.

Afternoon: Arrive at Denali, where you may enjoy a picturesque bus excursion deep into the park. Keep a lookout for grizzly bears, caribou, and, if you're fortunate, the elusive wolf.

Evening: Enjoy a calm night at a lodge within the park, with Denali, North America's tallest mountain, as your background.

Day 3: Gazing at the Northern Lights

Morning: Take a leisurely morning trek around the park, appreciating its natural beauty

Afternoon: Return to Anchorage and prepare for a spectacular evening chasing the Northern Lights. Head to an approved viewing place, where the dark Alaskan sky frequently comes alive with this stunning natural phenomenon.

Day 4: Idyllic Kenai Peninsula

Morning: Travel to the Kenai Peninsula, noted for its lush surroundings and maritime charm.

Afternoon: Explore the picturesque town of Seward and visit the Alaska SeaLife Center, where you may witness marine life up close.

Evening: Enjoy a wonderful seafood meal while staring out over the gorgeous Resurrection Bay.

Day 5: Wildlife Encounters in Seward

Morning: Embark on a wildlife and glacier cruise from Seward. Witness the rugged beauty of the Kenai Fjords, observe whales, puffins, and sea otters, and wonder at tidewater glaciers.

Afternoon: Hike the Exit Glacier Trail for a close experience with a glacier.

Evening: Return to Anchorage for a quiet evening in the city.

Day 6: Fairbanks Exploration

Morning: Catch a flight to Fairbanks, the "Golden Heart of Alaska." Visit the University of Alaska's Museum of the North and experience the city's unique heritage.

Afternoon: Take a paddlewheel riverboat trip on the Chena River, where you'll acquire insights into Fairbanks' gold rush history.

Evening: Don't miss the opportunity to watch the Northern Lights again in this northern city.

Day 7: Return to Anchorage

Morning: Before leaving Fairbanks, visit the Large Animal Research Station to witness musk oxen and caribou up close.

Afternoon: Fly back to Anchorage for your departure, but not before some last-minute shopping for Alaskan goods and mementos.

This 7-day adventure in Alaska gives a well-rounded perspective of the state's magnificent natural beauty, animal encounters, and cultural experiences. Each day is loaded with unforgettable events, ensuring your vacation to the Last Frontier is one you'll enjoy forever.

Chapter 12: Practical Essentials

Planning a vacation to Alaska demands a little more planning owing to its unique difficulties and distant locations. Here's a list of practical needs to guarantee a smooth and pleasurable journey:

1. Weather-Appropriate Clothing: Alaska's weather may be unpredictable. Pack layers, waterproof coats, and strong, comfy shoes. Don't forget warm gloves, a cap, and extra socks.

2. Bear Safety Gear: Alaska is a bear country. Carry bear spray, make noise on paths, and know how to respond if you meet one. Local counsel is crucial.

3. Mosquito Repellent: Alaskan mosquitoes are extremely tenacious. Bring bug repellant to fight off these small nuisances.

4. Travel Insurance: A comprehensive travel insurance package is a great decision. It covers emergencies, travel cancellations, and unforeseen situations.

5. Travel Adapter: Alaska utilizes Type A and B electrical outlets. Ensure you have the proper adaptor for your devices.

6. Outdoor Gear: If you want to indulge in outdoor activities, such as hiking or kayaking, rent or acquire the essential gear ahead to save time and money.

7. Maps and GPS: Despite technological developments, a good old-fashioned map or GPS gadget is necessary, particularly in isolated places.

8. First Aid Kit: Carry a basic first aid kit with necessities including bandages, pain relievers, and any personal prescriptions.

9. Snacks and Water: Alaska's vast terrain might imply lengthy distances between amenities. Have snacks and a refillable water bottle with you.

10. Local cash: While credit cards are commonly accepted, having some local cash on hand is important, particularly in small towns.

11. Binoculars and Camera: Alaska's animals and stunning sights are second to none. Binoculars and a great camera will improve your experience.

12. Campground Reservations: If camping is part of your vacation, make reservations in advance, particularly in popular places.

13. Emergency Contacts: Store emergency contact numbers, including local authorities, on your phone and a paper copy.

14. Bear-Proof Food Containers: If camping or trekking in bear-prone locations, take bear-proof containers for food storage.

15. Tides timetable: If you're visiting coastal places, know the tide timetable. In certain regions, it might alter fast.

By keeping these practical needs in mind, you'll be well-prepared to enjoy the breathtaking scenery and unique experiences that Alaska has to offer.

Money Matters and Gratuities in Alaska

Alaska is a unique tourist location, and knowing its monetary and tipping conventions is vital for a successful and polite visit.

Currency: The United States Dollar (USD) is the official currency of Alaska. Credit and debit cards are generally accepted in cities and towns, however, it's good to carry extra cash for areas that may not have card capabilities.

ATMs: Alaska has a large network of ATMs, making it easier for travelers to withdraw cash. You'll find ATMs in metropolitan places, although they may be less widespread in distant locations.

Tipping Customs: Tipping in Alaska follows a similar pattern to the rest of the United States. It's normal to tip service sector personnel, including waitstaff, tour guides, and hotel staff. **Here are some broad guidelines:**

Restaurants: A normal gratuity in restaurants is 15% to 20% of the entire cost before taxes. If you experience great service, consider leaving a higher tip.

Bartenders: When ordering drinks in a bar, tipping $1 to $2 per drink is common.

Hotel Staff: If a hotel doesn't include gratuity in the bill, consider paying housekeeping $2 to $5 each night.

Bellhops and concierge services should get $2 to $5 for each service.

Tour Guides: For guided tours and excursions, gratuity is recommended. The fee might vary based on the duration and style of the trip but normally runs from $5 to $10 per participant.

Taxis and Shuttle Drivers: A normal gratuity is 10% to 15% of the fare.

Gratuity Precautions: It's always a good habit to check your bill to verify that a gratuity hasn't already been applied, particularly at bigger places and for larger groups.

Credit Cards and Payment: Credit and debit cards are commonly accepted across Alaska. Even smaller establishments frequently accept cards, but it's still a good idea to carry extra cash in case you visit rural or distant places where cash may be preferred.

money Exchange: If you're visiting from outside the United States, you may exchange foreign money at banks and currency exchange offices in major Alaskan cities like Anchorage and Fairbanks. However, it's advisable to come with some US dollars on hand for emergency costs.

Banks and Exchange Services: Alaska has various banks and credit unions that provide currency exchange services, however rates and fees may vary. It's good to compare rates and verify whether your home bank has cooperated with Alaskan banks to cut expenses.

By understanding the currency, tipping customs, and payment methods in Alaska, you'll be well-prepared to navigate the financial aspects of your journey and ensure that you show appreciation for the great service you receive throughout your travels in the Last Frontier.

Staying Healthy in the Last Frontier

Alaska's magnificent scenery and unique experiences make it a fantastic vacation destination, but keeping healthy throughout your trip is crucial to properly appreciate this wildness.

1. Preparing for Your Trip

Travel Insurance: Consider investing in travel insurance that covers medical emergencies, including evacuation from distant regions.

Health Check: Before your travel, consult your healthcare professional for a routine check-up. Discuss your vacation intentions and any necessary vaccines.

2. Altitude Considerations: Some regions of Alaska are at high heights, such as Denali National Park. If you have altitude-related health issues, visit your doctor for guidance on acclimatization and treatments.

3. **Weather Awareness:** Alaska's climate may be unpredictable. Dress in layers, carry waterproof gear and be prepared for rapid weather changes to prevent hypothermia.

4. **Hydration:** Dehydration is a typical concern, particularly if you're indulging in outdoor activities. Carry a reusable water bottle and drink often, particularly in dry or cold circumstances.

5. **Preventing animal Encounters:** Alaska is abounding in animals. Stay a safe distance from animals, especially bears and moose. Bear-resistant food containers are vital in bear territory.

6. **Food Safety:** Enjoy local cuisine but emphasize food safety. Check the cleanliness of eateries, wash your hands often, and ensure meat and shellfish are fully cooked.

7. **Sun Protection:** Even during the midnight sun, Alaska's sun may be powerful. Use sunscreen, wear

sunglasses, and consider sun-protective gear, particularly if you're on the water.

8. Health Facilities: In big cities like Anchorage, Fairbanks, and Juneau, you'll find well-equipped hospitals and clinics. In remote locations, medical services may be limited. Familiarize oneself with the local healthcare facilities before going to rural places.

9. Emergency Services: Alaska's isolated locales might offer issues for emergency response. Carry a satellite phone, or GPS, and let someone know your trip intentions. In case of emergency, phone 911 if you have service.

10. Mosquito Protection: Alaskan mosquitoes may be strong, particularly during the summer. Bring bug repellent, long-sleeved clothes, and a mosquito head net if you're in mosquito-prone locations.

11. Medication and First-Aid Kit: If you take certain prescriptions, ensure you bring enough quantity for your trip. A basic first-aid kit with necessities like bandages, pain medications, and disinfectant wipes is also recommended.

12. Drinking Water: In isolated regions, tap water may not be drinkable. Carry water filtration equipment or boil water as required.

13. Bear Safety: In bear territory, understand bear habits and carry bear deterrents like bear spray. Hike in groups, make noise to avoid surprise bears, and store food carefully.

By taking care, being aware of your surroundings, and respecting the local environment and animals, you may appreciate the beauty of Alaska while guaranteeing your health and safety during your tour of the Last Frontier.

Conclusion

As your Alaskan trip draws to a conclusion, it's a fantastic moment to reflect on the incredible experiences you've had in the Last Frontier. Alaska has left an unforgettable impact on your heart, with its breathtaking vistas, fantastic animals, and rich cultural tapestry.

A Journey to Remember

Your tour in Alaska has been filled with awe-inspiring experiences, from gazing upon the Northern Lights to witnessing gorgeous whales in their native environment. You've traveled through beautiful wilderness, experienced the wealth of Alaskan waters, and toured attractive old villages. The memories produced here are yours to cherish.

Responsible Travel: Throughout your travels, you've maintained the ideals of responsible tourism, respecting the environment and local communities. By doing so, you've helped the preservation of this great country for decades to come.

A New Perspective: Alaska has a special way of altering people who encounter its immensity. It's a location that invites you to detach from the mundane and reconnect with the natural environment. Your trip has undoubtedly given you a fresh perspective on the beauty and fragility of our world.

The Spirit of Alaska

The individuals you've encountered along the road, from the enthusiastic natives to other tourists, have shared in your trip. This feeling of community is one of the genuine marvels of Alaska.

A Continuation of Your Tale: Though your formal Alaskan journey may have ended, the experiences and lessons you've received here will continue to define your life's tale. It's a location that has a way of luring you back, and maybe this isn't farewell but "until next time." Remember, an Alaskan experience is not simply a one-time excursion; it's a lasting link with a region that captures the spirit of exploration and the beauty of nature. As you leave Alaska, take with you the spirit of adventure, the appreciation for our planet's beauty, and the memories of a lifetime.

Made in United States
Troutdale, OR
01/07/2024

16776452R00086